Jonas Lauritz Idemil Lie, Jessie Muir

One of Life's Slaves

Jonas Lauritz Idemil Lie, Jessie Muir

One of Life's Slaves

ISBN/EAN: 9783744713269

Printed in Europe, USA, Canada, Australia, Japan

Cover: Foto ©Thomas Meinert / pixelio.de

More available books at **www.hansebooks.com**

ONE OF LIFE'S SLAVES

BY

JONAS LIE

AUTHOR OF "THE VISIONARY," ETC. ETC.

TRANSLATED FROM THE NORWEGIAN

BY JESSIE MUIR

LONDON

HODDER BROTHERS

18 NEW BRIDGE STREET, E.C.

1895

PREFACE

In a review which appeared in the *Athenæum*, of a translation of one of Jonas Lie's earlier works—"Den Fremsynte" ("The Visionary")—the reviewer expressed a hope that I would follow up that translation with "an English version of Lie's 'Livsslaven,' that intensely tragic and pathetic story of suffering and wrong." It is in accordance with this suggestion that the present volume makes its appearance.

In taking Christiania life for the subject of "Livsslaven," Jonas Lie attempted for the second time to break down the preconceived opinion of critics, that such a subject did not come within his province. They were accustomed to have tales of sea-life from his pen, and could not readily be persuaded that another sphere of life might afford equal scope for his talent. "Thomas Ross," published in 1878, had treated of Christiania life, and had attracted but little attention; and now, in the spring of 1883, appeared this "story of a smith's apprentice, with his struggles for existence and his ultimate final failure owing to the irresistible indulgence of a passionate physical instinct." At first this too seemed to be a failure. To use the words of Arne Garborg, a Norwegian author and critic, Lie "had spoken—cried out in the passion or agony of his soul, and people stood there quite calm and as if they had heard nothing;" there seemed to be a total lack of sympathetic comprehension on the part of the public. In the end, however, the book found its way to the hearts of its readers, and, to quote Mr. Gosse's words on the subject, "achieved a very great success; it was realistic and modern in a certain sense and to a discreet degree, and it appealed, as scarcely any Norwegian novel had done before, to all classes of Scandinavian society."

Lie himself, in speaking of this work, says that a writer should "aim at presenting his subject in such a way that the reader may see, hear, feel, and comprehend it with the utmost possible intensity." This precept he has certainly put into practice in the present instance, for the subject is treated with such power and so full a grasp, that in reading the book one feels an actual anxiety, an oppression as of approaching disaster. This, at any rate, is the case with the original, and I trust that its power has not been altogether lost in the process of rendering into another language, but that the stamp of genuineness, the author's leading characteristic, may to some extent be found also in this translation.

J. MUIR.

CHRISTIANIA,
November 10, 1894.

CONTENTS

ONE OF LIFE'S SLAVES

CHAPTER I

NEGLECTED RESPONSIBILITIES

"LIKE a prince in his cradle," you say, "with invisible fairies and the innocent peace of childhood over him!"

What fairy stood by the cradle of Barbara's Nikolai it would be difficult to say. Out at the tinsmith's, in the little house with the cracked and broken window-panes in the outskirts of the town, there was often a run of visitors, generally late at night, when wanderers on the high road were at a loss for a night's lodging. Many a revel had been held there, and it was not once only that the cradle had been overturned in a fight, or that a drunken man had fallen full length across it.

Nikolai's mother was called Barbara, and came from Heimdalhögden, somewhere far up in the country—a genuine mountain lass, shining with health, red and white, strong and broad-shouldered,

and with teeth like the foam in the milk pail. She
had heard so much about the town from cattle-
dealers that came over the mountain, that a longing
and restlessness had taken possession of her.

And then she had gone out to service in the
town.

She was about as suitable there as a tumble-down
haystack in a handsome town street, or as a cow on
a flight of stairs—that is to say, not at all.

She used to waste her time on the market-place
by all the hay loads. She must see and feel the hay
—*that* was not at all like mountain grass. "No
indeed! Mountain grass was so soft, and then, how
it smelt! Oh dear no!"

But her mistress had other uses for her servant
than letting her spend the morning talking to hay-
cart drivers. So she went from place to place, each
time descending both as regarded wages and mistress.
Barbara was good-natured and honest; but she had
one fault—the great one of being totally unfit for all
possible town situations.

Yet Society has, as we know, a wonderful
faculty for making use of, assimilating and recon-
structing everything, even the apparently most
meaningless and useless, for its own purpose. And
the way it took, quickly enough, with poor Barbara
was that she became the only thing in which she
could be of any service in the town—namely, a
nurse.

It was a sad time and a hard struggle while the

shame lasted, almost enough to kill her; and after that, she never thought of returning to the Heimdal mountains again.

But things were to be still harder.

The various social claims, which an age of progress increasingly lays upon the lady of the house in the upper classes of society, asserted themselves here in the town by an ever increasing demand for nurses.

"The reason," as Dr. Schneibel explained, "was simply a law of Nature—you can't be a milch-cow and an intelligent human being at the same time. The renovation of blood and nerves must be artificially conveyed from that class of society which stands nearer to Nature."

And now the thing was to find an extra-healthy, thoroughly strong nurse for Consul-General Veyergang's two delicate, newly-arrived, little ones.

Dr. Schneibel had very thoughtfully kept a nurse in reserve for Mrs. Veyergang—"a really remarkable specimen of the original healthiness in the common stock. One might say—h'm, h'm—that if Mrs. Veyergang could not get to the mountains, the mountains were so courteous as to come to her. The girl still had an odour of the cowshed about her perhaps; but when all's said and done, that was only a stronger assurance of originality. And *that* is an important factor in our day, madam, when milk is adulterated even from the very cows themselves.— Quite young, scarcely twenty!"

Barbara Högden had not the faintest suspicion, as she carried water and wood, or stood at the edge of the ice beating linen, or did any drudgery she could find to do, in order to earn a little money to pay for herself and her baby at the tinsmith's, that, from her deepest degradation, she had risen at one step to the rank of an exceptionally sought-after and esteemed person in the town.

For a nurse *is* an esteemed person. Indeed, she is on the expectancy list to become respected.

After having nursed her mistress's child, and been a correspondingly unnatural mother to her own, she ends by sleeping on down, and being considered in every way, until a new nurse for a new heir deposes her from her dynasty.

Should she prefer to give her own little baby the only treasure she possesses, her healthy breast, should she really be so blind to her own interests, why then the case is different, and (to use Dr. Schneibel's words) not altogether unmerited, only a result of the social economy to which she does not know how to be intelligently subordinate, and which will reduce her, with the inexorable logic of the laws of civilisation, to a useless superfluity, which Society's organism rejects. Or, vulgarly speaking, she is left with shame, contempt and poverty resting upon both her and her illegitimate offspring. As a private individual, she is in a sense right; but socially, as a member of society——!

At first poor Barbara was quite blind on this

point, utterly obstinate, rigid as a mountain pony that could not be got to stir.

Dr. Schneibel was standing for the third time at the tinsmith's, with his stick under his nose, while his gig waited down in the road. Each time he had added to both wages and arguments, and had again and again pointed out how bad it would be both for her and her boy if she continued so obstinate. He appealed to her own good sense. How could she expect to bring him up in such poor, narrow circumstances, and with all this toiling and moiling? She would only need to give up a part of her large wages to the tinsmith, and they would look well after the boy. Besides she could often come out and see him, at least once a month!—he could promise her that on the Veyergangs' behalf, and it was very kind of them now they lived such a long way out of town.

Dr. Schneibel talked both kindly and severely, both good-naturedly and sharply: he was almost like a father.

Barbara felt a pang of fear every time she saw him come down the street, and turn in by the rotten, mouldy wooden fence. She watched him like a bird that is afraid for her nest, and was sitting close to the wall in the darkest corner with the cradle behind her, when he opened the door. It was impossible for her to answer except by a sob. The tinsmith's wife did all the talking with: "Why, bless me, yes!" and "Bless me, no!" and "Just so, doctor!" in

garrulous superabundance, while Barbara only sat
and meditated on taking her baby on her back and
departing.

But to-day the doctor had talked so very kindly to
her and offered her so much money. He had
appealed so directly to her conscience, patted the
child, and said that when it came to the point,
he was sure she was not the mother who could
be so cruel as to bring misery upon such a pretty
little fellow, let him suffer want, let his pretty
little feet be cold, when he might lie both comfortable and warm and like a little prince in his
cradle !

It was not possible to resist, and in her emotion
something like a half promise escaped her.

Afterwards a neighbour came in and was of
exactly the same opinion, and told of all the little
children whom she had known that had died of want
and neglect, only in the houses round about, during
the last two years, because their mothers had had to
go out and work all day and could not pay any one to
look after them. And she and the tinsmith's wife
both spoke at once about the same thing—only the
same thing.

Barbara sat listening and tending her child. Her
heart felt like breaking. For a moment she thought
of going, not to Högden, but in another way, home
with him at once.

It was a temptation.

That night she broke into sobs so ungovernable,

that, in order not to disturb the household in their slumbers, she went out into the soft, drizzling rain: it quieted and cooled her.

As she was standing the next morning, helping a neighbour's wife to rinse and wring the clothes by the brook, a pony-carriage stopped in the road. The coachman—he had gold lace on his hat and coat—got down and went in to the tinsmith's.

"You must wring that sheet right out, Barbara," said the neighbour's wife; "it'll be the last you'll wring here, for that's the Consul's carriage."

And Barbara wrung the sheet until there was not a drop of water in it. It had come now!

She went in and dressed the child; she hardly knew what she was doing, and hardly felt it under her hands.

She saw the man give six dollars to the tinsmith's wife. He was so stiff and tall and distinguished-looking, with such a big, aristocratic nose, and he made a kind of bend every time she happened to look at him, and assured her that there was no hurry—not the least! They never woke before nine at the Consul's, so there was still plenty of time, And then he looked at his watch.

And every time he looked at his watch, she looked at her boy: there were now orders and a time fixed for her to leave him.

He had fallen asleep again. If he were to wake, she did not know what would happen—she was sure she could not leave him then.

"No hurry, no hurry!" and he took the thick silver watch out of his pocket once more.

But now it was she who was in a hurry, and so eager that she gave herself no time to look round before she was seated in the carriage, and the long, stiff-necked, braided coachman was driving her away along the road of her appointed destiny.

In the summer she accompanied the Consul-General's family to a bathing-place. There Barbara wheeled the perambulator with the two children in it along the shore, and more than once the Veyer-gangs were flattered by the exclamations of passers-by: "What a fine-looking nurse!"

But there were difficulties with her, too—fits of melancholy to which she completely gave way. She would sit by the cradle, her eyes red with weeping, longing for her child, and would neither eat nor drink.

This was a matter of no little importance. A nurse must be kept in good spirits; her frame of mind has such an immense influence on her health, and that again on the health of the child.

Mrs. Veyergang had all sorts of good things brought in from the pastry-cook's to enliven her; silk hand-kerchiefs and aprons abounded, and the servants at home received injunctions to inquire after Barbara's boy at the tinsmith's.

There was praise and nothing but praise to be given every time the Consul-General's Lars stopped there in driving past, and when Barbara only received a message of that kind, she could be happy and contented the whole month.

She was made much of, as she very soon felt. If she said or wanted anything, she was obeyed as if she were the mistress herself. And handsome clothes with constant change of fine underclothing, not to mention meat and drink—hardly anything of what she was accustomed to call work, her hands had already become quite soft and supple. And she felt that she was beginning to be attached to the two little ones whom she tended day and night.

One day, after the Consul's family had returned from the bathing-place, Barbara set out for the tin-smith's. It was late in the autumn. She could hardly ever remember the road out there so bad and muddy as it was now. Both her boots and the bottom of her dress would need cleaning and washing when she got back again.

The thought that she would soon see her boy put her in a cold perspiration ; but of course things were best as they were, now that she could pay so well for him.

When she turned in by the wooden fence and saw the cottage with its familiar cracked windows in front of her, she slackened her pace a little. A feeling of apprehension suddenly came over her.

And then the neighbour's wife, whom she had so often helped, came out and began to talk and give her information, rattling on like a steam-engine. There had been war among the neighbours in the tinsmith's alley, and now that she saw Barbara herself, the truth should out, the real, actual truth.

The tinsmith's people need not imagine that other people hadn't got eyes in their head! Everything they possessed had gone to the pawnbroker's; there was barely enough of the tin-ware left to put in his cracked windows. And what they lived on, nobody round there could imagine, unless it was the payment they got for that poor little ill-used boy, that they gave lager-beer to, to keep him quiet. For no one would put up there now that the police had begun to keep an eye on the company, not even certain people who were not generally so particular about their quarters.

" But if you take my advice, Barbara, you'll take the boy to blockmaker Holman's down at the wharf. They are such nice, respectable people, and have pitied the boy so when I told them how they were treating him out here."

Blockmaker Holman, blockmaker Holman! The name rang in her ears as, heavy-hearted, she entered the tinsmith's.

There he lay among the ragged, dirty clothes, pale, thin and neglected, with frightened eyes. He began to cry when she took him up; he did not know her, and she scarcely knew him.

The disappointment—all that she felt—found vent in a rising torrent of angry words against the tinsmith and his wife.

But at the same time, while she was washing the

boy, she felt how big, coarse and clumsy his face and body were, compared to the two delicate ones she was accustomed to. She saw now for the first time how impossible it would be to keep him herself.

But he should go to the blockmaker's, poor boy! Her name wasn't Barbara if she didn't get her mistress to see to that at once—as early as to-morrow.

She returned home with a face red and swollen with crying, and was inconsolable the whole evening until her mistress came down from the office with the promise that the matter should be arranged.

And thus it was that Nikolai came to block-maker Holman's.

CHAPTER II

A STRICT DISCIPLINARIAN

It is in some ways a blessing that those who have suffered hardship and been neglected in their baby-hood, do not remember anything about it—and yet perhaps something clings to them.

So, at any rate, Mrs. Holman declared. From the very first day the boy came into the house, she could see he had been brought up in a thieves' nest. His eyes were so wise and watchful, and he could be so craftily cunning and refractory, long before he could speak. She declared that he was positively malicious, so drowsy and quiet as he would be until she had just fallen asleep, when he would begin to shout as loud as a watchman.

But every one who knew anything about the Holmans, said that if they had not been fortunate in getting the boy, he had at any rate been fortunate in having found his way to them. There were not two opinions as to what an orderly woman Mrs. Holman was, and how strict in the fulfilment of her duty. Tall, thin and neat in her person, even her small, liver-coloured face, with the pale blue

expressionless eyes, told you at once that she was
not the woman to allow herself to be carried away
by rash impetuosity.

And on the few occasions in the year that
Barbara visited the boy—it was not so easy for her
to come now that the Veyergangs lived in their
country house all the year round—she could see for
herself how well-cared-for and clean he was, and
how strictly he was kept. From the time she got
there to the time she left, she heard nothing except
how difficult it was to straighten out all the tinsmith's dents, all that had been wrongly and
improperly dealt with from the very first, especially his obstinate temper! Now he really could
walk quite a good way, but he would do nothing
but crawl, and so quickly, that no sooner had she,
Mrs. Holman, taken her eyes off him than he might
be anywhere, either at the saucepans and pots, or in
the water-bucket, or else at the plummets on the
bell. And he upset things, and got himself in a
mess, wherever he went; yesterday the cat's food
lay all over the floor! So now she had hung the
birch-rod low down on the wall, so that it might be
before his eyes; for it was necessary to frighten
him, and vigilance and punishment must positively
be used. And Barbara must know herself, that it
wasn't so easy to manage other people's children,
and especially such a stray creature, come into
the world in such a manner!

It was all just, as Barbara was obliged to acknowledge to herself, from beginning to end, however much it might sting her, and therefore she was always in a hurry to get away again.

It cannot be denied that she learnt something from it too, namely, what she, on her side, might have reason and right to say to Mrs. Veyergang about all the toil she had had with her two, if they ever had a difference.

But the same spirit of disobedience remained in the boy as he grew older. It was impossible to cure him of it, for all that Mrs. Holman could do, and Holman had to help too sometimes. This did not happen, however, until his wife had duly impressed on him the moral necessity of taking upon himself his share of the duties of the house.

Holman was a silent man with a pair of quiet, shining eyes. He went and came, morning and evening, rubbed and dried his shoes, and stood hesitating at the door with some tool or other, or the tail of a block in his hand, before he went in. What he might think of his married life there was little opportunity of seeing in his face. One thing was certain—a wife like Mrs. Holman was a treasure, which could not be sufficiently prized; and if there was not quite so much left of Holman, if, in fact, he had become—with all reverence be it said—something of a fool, yet every one was sensible that in that union it must be so, if the balance was to be kept. Any one who had only seen or spoken to Mrs. Holman once, understood it immediately, but what was not so easy to understand was that, after all, it was Holman who made the blocks down in the workshop, by which the household lived.

It was still more remarkable that he had sometimes been met in the gateway in an irresponsible condition, such as no one would have expected in a man so happily married as he was.

After the miracle of Mrs. Holman's having a little girl herself had happened—after that great and important change in the houshold, it was deliberated whether it would not be better to rid the room of other people's progeny. But then it was good regular money to have, and in time the boy could be made use of at the cradle.

It was the lightest work in the world—just made for a little boy, sitting and rocking the cradle with his foot—nothing but a little practice for him.

But here, too, she was to have sad experience. She left him by the cradle went she went out, but when she came home, he would be standing gazing out of the window or from the top of the cellar stairs at the children playing in the square. She had even caught him right outside with the door open behind him—it was all the same to him, as long as he could get out of the cellar and away from his duty.

Well, the young rogue would have to pay for it, as much as his mortal back could bear!

And she assured the servant upstairs, who put in her head to hear what the little imp had done now, as he was screaming so—that all the punishment she gave him, and all her attempts, both by letting him have no supper and by locking him in, were equally useless : he was just as defiant and unreliable as ever !

She had frightened him now by saying that the devil sat in the corner behind the bed and watched to see if he left the cradle !

He was almost beside himself with terror, and fancied all the time that he could see the aforesaid sinister personage putting up his head over Mrs. Holman's pillow. He could not help looking now and again towards the window—there was some one playing outside in the square. And, somehow or other, he came to be standing there, and stood until he once more remembered what was behind him. Then he darted back like an arrow, and sat staring in mortal fear into the corner.

From being made useful beside the cradle, Nicolai was advanced in course of time to mind the Holman's daughter Ursula, outside the cellar steps. To move farther, only as far as the trees over on the other side of the street, was a capital offence. The idea of what overstepping the bounds meant, was impressed upon him with full force. How could Mrs. Holman be sure otherwise that he did not take Silla right up to the basin round the fountain, where all the naughty boys played with their ships, and shouted and made a noise? His poor little body had received so many black and blue marks every time he had fallen into temptation that at last the limits stood instinctively before his frightened perception like an invisible iron grating   A foot's breadth beyond was, in his imagination, the blackest crime, an enormity which would draw down the fiercest retribution upon him.

That Silla was an uncommon and remarkable being of a higher order, so to speak, than himself, had been driven into him in so many ways ever since she came into the world, that he looked upon the assertion as raised above all doubt.

Notwithstanding everything that he had endured for her sake, or perhaps, by a strange contradiction, just because of these sufferings, the feeling that she was under his care was most highly developed. His admiration of her was unqualified; he thought her more than remarkable in her blue bow and an old red stuff rose in her hat, and he submitted to a wilfulness which was quite as despotic as even Mrs. Holman's. When he had sat long enough and let her fill his hair with dust, she would order him to pull off her shoes and stockings. If he did it, he got a beating; if he did not do it, she screamed, and then he got a beating too.

Insecurity was, so to speak, the soil on which he lived, and the hurried, shrinking glances he continually cast, as if from habit, towards the cellar door—even when his often guilt-laden conscience felt itself most guiltless—were only the fruit of daily experience.

B

"You could see the bad conscience in his face, a long way off," said Mrs. Holman; and it was true— the quick, watchful look up with the grey eyes was to see what sins he was guilty of now.

"Good neighbours and other good things," the catechism says. But in our times we have no neighbours; you do not know who lives on the floor above you or on the floor below, or even on the other side of the passage. And so it was that no one in the house had any ear to speak of for Nikolai's various untoward fortunes below in the cellar, although their character often asserted itself with no uncertain sound during their execution.

The neighbours had become accustomed to the continual screaming and howling of that naughty boy, just as one accustoms one's self to piano practising or the din of a factory; perhaps too, they comforted themselves with the thought that it was most fortunate that such a morally depraved child had come under discipline and correction.

When Nikolai and Silla wandered as usual up and down the pavement outside the cellar, the people of the house might often in passing give the little girl a friendly nod. To give Nikolai any encouragement in that way would have been a mistake.

Maren, the cook, who had come to the floor above last hiring-day,* had naturally no conception of Mrs.

* The days for changing servants in Norway are in the spring and autumn. In Christiana they are the second Friday after Easter, and the second Friday after Michaelmas.

Holman's strict, conscientious character, and was therefore to be excused in what now took place.

She went down into the cellar with the lantern one evening to fetch coal and wood, panting and puffing down the stairs as she used to do; she had a bend in both hips from rheumatism, and rocked from one side to the other like a boat's mast in rough weather.

From the wood-cellar she all at once heard a sound as of wailing in the darkness within. It was as though some one were crying, and now and again sobbing convulsively for some time without being able to produce a distinct sound.

The voice sounded so utterly broken-hearted that Maren stopped putting the wood into her apron and stood by the chopping-block listening. It seemed to come from one of the coal cellars up the dark passage. At last she seized the lantern and groped her way in; she must come to the bottom of this.

" Is any one here?" she cried at the door whence the sobbing came.

There was a sudden complete silence.

She knocked hard with a bit of wood, but then from within there came a terrified scream, which made Maren drop the wood from her apron and pull open the hasp of the door which was fastened with a piece of wood.

"But who has put the poor little boy in here— in the pitch black darkness?"

By the light of the lantern she saw Nikolai staring at her in wild terror.

"I thought it was the devil, I did. Yes, for he does knock on the wall."

"Oh, you'd frighten any one out of their senses, boy, with those ugly words!"

"Mrs. Holman says so;" and with a quick, inquiring glance up at Maren he added, "but do you think she only says it so that I shan't touch her sugar?"

"Is that what you are here for?"

"I haven't taken anything from her, but I will, if she says it whether I do or not! It was only that Monday when I put my tongue down into the bag and licked when I'd gone for half a pound. But now I'll crunch it so that she'll only have the empty bag left! I'll take! I'll steal!" he added and ground his teeth. "Don't—don't go!' he sobbed, catching hold of her dress, "for when it's dark again, he'll come and take me!"

What was Maren to do? She stood hesitating and considering; she dare not let the boy out.

She might try and beg him off from Mrs. Holman.

"Only get me another beating for that, too!" was the answer.

There was nothing else for it; she could not let the poor little frightened thing stay there in the coal-hole. So, with eyes closed to the consequences of her own determination, she exclaimed:

" Then you must come up into the kitchen with
me, and sleep on the bench there to-night."

This time, Nikolai did not weigh the probabilities
of what Mrs. Holman would say or do ; he only took
hold of her skirt with both hands. And with the
boy close in her wake, Maren sailed up the kitchen
stairs again.

While she was looking out some of her old
shawls and skirts to put under him, taking some
of the clothes from her own bed, and making it
as comfortable and warm as she could for him on
the bench, Nikolai seemed to have forgotten all his
troubles.

There was so much that was new up here. There
were such a number of shining tin things hanging
all over the wall, and then the cat was an old friend.
He had seen it many a time down in the yard, and
now he had to squeeze himself together to get hold
of it, it had crept so far under the bed.

There ! He had knocked down the tin kettle with
his back !

He fled in terror to the door. But Maren picked
it up quite quietly ; there was not a word of scold-
ing, a thing he wondered more at than either the
tin things or the cat.

Maren had at last fallen asleep after all the
aching and pain of the rheumatism in her weary
joints, with which she always had to contend at the
beginning of the night. She was awakened by a
wild shriek.

"What is it—what is it, Nikolai? Nikolai!"

She lighted the bit of candle. He was sitting up, fencing with his arms.

"I thought they were going to take my head off," he explained, when he at length collected himself.

When she lay down again, Maren could not help thinking how glad she was that she had no child to be responsible for. Every one has his trouble, and now she had this rheumatism.

But it was a shock to her, when, on the kitchen stairs next morning, in the presence of the servants both from the other side of the passage and from the first floor, Mrs. Holman called her to account for having interfered in what was none of her business. She then received such full information, once for all, both as to why Mrs. Holman had shut him in, and what they had to go through daily with that boy, that Maren was completely nonplussed. For this Mrs. Holman could stake her life upon, that if there was any one in the house who could not stand disorder or unseemly behaviour, it was she. She could not imagine a worse punishment than to have it said of her that she allowed shame and depravity to flourish in her sight.

But when Maren sat down there in the evening by the lantern on the chopping-block, and could hear the boy screaming right from the Holmans' room, she was not capable of going upstairs until the worst was over. She thought she had never heard anything so heart-rending, even though it was in the cause of justice.

Up with Maren was a kind of harbour of refuge for the boy. He would sit there as quiet as a mouse in the corner by the wood-box, carving himself boats, which he put under his blouse when he carried Holman's dinner down to the workshop near the quay.

To represent, however, that Nikolai's existence was passed, so to speak, in the coal-cellar, or under blows on back and ear from Mrs. Holman's warm hands, would be an exaggeration. He had also his palmy days, when Mrs. Holman overflowed with words of praise—praise, if not exactly of him, yet of everything that she had accomplished in her daily toil for his moral improvement.

Twice a year she had to call for the payment for him at the Consul-General's office in the town. Nikolai, too, often had leave to go out to the country house with the kitchen cart, which had come in to make the morning purchases.

And there he would sit, while the cart rumbled and jolted along the road, smart and clean, head and body respectively combed and scoured like a copper kettle that has been cleaned with sand and lye. He could not sit still a minute; he talked and asked questions—always about the horse, the wonderful brown horse—whether it was the best or the second best, if it could go faster than the railway train, or who and what it could beat.

Then the cart turned—so much too soon—into the yard in front of the kitchen door, and he was led through the passage by the man-servant to the nursery.

"I hope you have rubbed your shoes? You might have had the sense, Lars, not to bring the boy in that way, with such shoes as those!" His mother took him and set him on a chair.

And then he was given bread-and-butter and cracknels and milk. But he must wait now until she came in again, for she was busy to-day washing Lizzie's and Ludvig's clothes.

In rushed the aforesaid children, his equals in point of age; the one was drawing a large saddled horse after him, the other was carrying two large, dressed dolls. They had been sent out by their mother to play with Nikolai. And they were soon in full gallop round the nursery. Gee-up! gee-up!—Nikolai drew, and Ludvig rode—hi! gee-up! And at last Nikolai wanted to ride too; he had been drawing for such a long time. But Ludvig would not get down, so Nikolai dropped the bridle and pulled him off the horse by one leg.

" You ragged boy! How dare you? "

" Ragged boy! Ragged boy yourself! " It ended with a fling up on to the bed, behind which Ludvig entrenched himself howling, while his sister took his part and joined in.

" What is the matter, what is the matter, dears? " cried Barbara, hurrying in. " Aren't you ashamed of yourself, Nikolai, behaving like that to the Consul's children! You'd better try it on! There Ludvig — there, there, Lizzie — he shan't hurt you! Just do what they want, do you hear, Nikolai!"

And then Barbara had to lament over Ludvig's starched collar, which had got crumpled.

"Come here, my precious boy. Come now, and then you shall play again directly."

She took him up on her knee. "It's my own precious boy, it is, who's so good! There, hold his blouse, Nikolai, and you shall see such a fine boy, and so good, so good!"

"Show him my Sunday clothes, Barbara, and the patent leather shoes!" And Nikolai was allowed to look into the drawers at all Ludvig's and Lizzie's dresses and sashes and fine underclothes, and to peep into the toy-cupboard to be bewildered by all the old drums and trumpets and headless men and horses, and tin soldiers, and Noah's arks, with their belongings, all of which, Barbara said, they had been given because they were so good.

There was a pile of things in the lower part of the cupboard, so that Nikolai could understand that they must have been very, very good, and that his mother, too—and at this he felt a bitter disappointment—must, in return, be very, very fond of them. They must be very different children to what he was, if they never deserved a whipping, but always playthings. He became quite tired and downcast, as

he stood there. If he ever met Ludvig anywhere,
he would pay him out about the horse.

At last the hour of departure arrived, when he was
to go with the pony-carriage that fetched the Consul
from town at three o'clock. The two children both
clung to his mother's skirt when she followed him out.

"Good-bye, Nikolai!" and she patted him in such
a way on the cheek and head that he looked at her
half doubtingly, "and give my respects to Holman
and Mrs. Holman. Do you hear? Whatever you
do, don't forget Mrs. Holman. And—I declare
you're kicking the varnish now! You must sit quite
still, Nikolai, the whole way. Don't you know that
you mustn't come near those fine carriage-cushions
with your boots? You should just see how nicely
Ludvig and Lizzie sit, when they go for a drive—
don't you, dears?"

And off he set.

It had indeed been a gala day, and he had been
given a large, sugared twist to take with him, and it
tasted delicious; but somehow or other he began to
cry all at once on the way home.

The next day he had full confirmation of how
delightful it had been.

While he was going up and down the pavement
in his daily occupation of taking care of Silla, he
caught fragments of Mrs. Holman's remarks to the
housekeeper up stairs, as they stood under the arch-
way; he never for a moment lost sight of her tall
figure.

"You may well say so, Miss Damm. Take him into the room with their own children; there aren't many grand folks that would have done such an honour to one like him.". . . "We must do so many things in this world, Miss Damm—we must scour the boards over the gutter, so to speak, and put up with them—and I don't mind saying that he showed that he was well cared-for from top to toe.". . . "Such an honour! It might have been some respectable child they had asked there. He ought to remember it the whole of his life!". . . "So grand as she is now, she doesn't much care about coming out here and acknowledging the boy. It's nothing for those that can pay to get rid of their shame!"

Nikolai crushed with all his might an old decapitated cock's head, which lay in the gutter, with the heel of his boot, until it was as flat as a penny.

When the terror of bogies and the devil in the coal-cellar had lost its power, one of Mrs. Holman's most powerful means of keeping Nikolai in order was a threat of sending him to the parish school—an institution which stood before her imagination as a publicly authorised house of correction for youth, and a daily training-ground in the fulfilment of one's duty.

He never obtained any very clear idea of what would happen when he went to school; but that it was something quite indeterminably dreadful was evident from the constantly renewed disguised hints, and the repressed, mystical groans and nods by which they were accompanied.

One day the threat was really carried out: he was to go next Monday morning.

Thursday, Friday, Saturday and Sunday, he counted on his fingers — he had all those days left. And how he took care of and played with Silla during them, and darted on errands like an arrow!

At last there was only the Sunday afternoon left.

He sat at tea-time with Silla and tried to take comfort from her opinions about school, heard that he was to have his Sunday clothes on to-morrow too, because it was the first time, and fell asleep that night with drops of perspiration on his forehead.

In the morning Nikolai was not to be found.

Mrs. Holman inquired, and sought, and called, promising liberally both torments and pardon if he would only come at once; but it was all of no use, he had vanished.

After dinner Maren upstairs was startled by seeing him emerge from under her bed. She gave him some food and asked him to promise to go home; and Nikolai said he would, only not before it was dark.

In the twilight he made an excursion down to the quay, where he amused himself for an hour by sitting and rocking in a ship's boat; then in the wet October darkness he slunk through the narrow, dripping passages between the warehouses, until he was sure that there was no longer any light on the square, and spent the rest of the evening lying peeping over the paling at the light in the two cellar windows at home. He noticed how Holman came slinking cautiously up and stood a little while at the door before going in, and how they put Silla to bed. The light from the windows told him, like two dimly-glaring, merciless eyes, that if he came home now, the well-merited sentence of justice would most certainly be carried out.

Then the light was put out.

Through the drizzling rain late that night the gleam of a lantern glanced among the stacks of wet planks, and behind it was a pair of eyes which were accustomed to look in the dark for all kinds of persons who might think fit to hide themselves in the yard. The lantern wandered about among the narrow rows, sometimes standing still, while it threw its searching, reddish light as far as possible in between the planks.

No one was discovered that night. Among the many square spaces which could give shelter, Nikolai, with a certain inborn instinct, had chosen the foremost and most unsuspicious looking one, which stood half built with a sloping plank-roof over it. There he lay wedged into the farthest corner, close wrapped in the happy Nirvana of self-forgetfulness—school zero, and Mrs. Holman a cipher—his body bent down over his knees, his coat pulled up about his neck to keep out the drips, and his boots down in the wet mud.

But that night under the wet sky, with Trondsen's planks for his bed-posts, brought something new into his mind, a feeling—showing certainly the greatest insensibility to all Mrs. Holman's solicitous care—that the timber-yard was really his home, a certain independent, free savage's consciousness in relation to everything that they might afterwards think fit to screw him into, the school no less than Mrs. Holman's cellar steps ; the planks in the timber-yard shone so white in bright weather, and when it grew dark, they stood there like his oft-tried, secret friends, who could screen him from the terrors at home.

He was taken to school, however, and one of his first timid, inquiring glances was to discover the thrashing-block with which Mrs. Holman had threatened him. He had pictured it to himself giving blow after blow with a rod, and beating incessantly, like the chicory factory at the bottom of the square.

Strangely enough there was no such block. But there were other things into which he was to be squeezed and forced like a last into a boot ; and he was a hard last, which often would not go farther than the leg, and had to be hammered and knocked the rest of the way, where others more pliable glided smoothly down like eels.

There were things he understood, and things he did not understand. The former did not often happen to be explained to him, the latter he did not understand however many explanations were given; the result was a painful consciousness, a continual difference or falling short both in relation to his lessons and his teachers, which had to be adjusted by the cane and detention, while the majority of his schoolmates, in this particular also, more supple, worked themselves out like true virtuosi.

But what was even a whole day at school, with its full measure of misfortunes, in comparison to the endlessly long, dull hours of the evening, when Mrs. Holman, with her own eyes, " watched over him, to see that he learnt his lessons," and he hardly dared so much as to glance across at Silla.

As to Holman, experience had taught them that his fixed and staring eyes saw nothing : he sat mute and quiet the whole evening. In Mrs. Selvig's tap-room he found a remedy which made him insensible to moral lectures even the most reasonable and impressive. There he stood every evening a quarter of an hour after working-hours, as regular as clock-work, and when the hands of the clock drew near to eight, he just as regularly set off homewards, a punctuality which, be it said in passing, had gained for him in the tap-room the title of *General with order.*

CHAPTER III

A FIGHT AND ITS CONSEQUENCES

THAT was a dangerous corner, where the wide street leading to the grammar school crossed the narrow one that led to the board school; and, on the days when the afternoon hours for the latter began just when the grammar school's long morning was over, it might happen that the free, exuberant spirits of those who were leaving school came into collision with the heavier and more bitter mood of those who were on their way to it.

Ludvig Veyergang, with his sealskin satchel on his back, had already travelled this road for several years. He had been nicknamed the Ostrich, because of his little head with the bird-like nose, his long bare neck, and the way he walked. When he met Nikolai, he pretended not to know him, and Nikolai whistled and clattered with his shoes on the pavement.

The board school's new slide ran along the gutter a good way out into the grammar school street. It was the product of the joint work of many for a whole week, and fate willed that Nikolai, at the head of a string of comrades, should come full speed down it, hallooing and shouting, just as Ludvig Veyergang and a few others came round the corner. Young Veyergang received a push that made him drop his pencil-case ; and pens, lead and slate pencils lay strewn over the ground.

"Pick them up, you beggar!" he cried to Nikolai, for it was he who had knocked up against him. "I shall tell about you at home, you may be pretty sure. Pick them up, or——"

A kick sent a few loose lumps of snow in answer.

"You shall be made to bend soon enough, if that's what you want. Father shall be told, this very day, that you are the leader of the street cads in the town ; and if no one else will tell your mother about it, I'll tell her myself, however much she cries!"

"Do you want to have your ostrich-beak pulled?"

"You'd better try it on! Perhaps you don't know that we pay for you at the blockmaker's. But I'll take care that you get thrashed until you beg my pardon : a fellow who doesn't even know who his father is, and his mother only wishes he had never been born!"

The last words were hardly out of his mouth when Nikolai sprang upon him with both fists like a pair of sledge-hammers, and for a few blissful seconds hammered out every trace of difference in birth and position. Now he should feel "both his father and his mother!"

It was one of the board school's memorable and famous days, when the wine was tapped from Ludvig Veyergang's nose in the snow; and even the next day at dinner-time, two or three school classes of interested spectators were searching for traces of red spots in the snow by the lamp-post.

But, though he enjoyed great honour and admiration during the whole afternoon at school, Nikolai knew that at home he would meet with an utterly different interpretation of the event, news of which the Holmans must already have received, surely and promptly, from the Veyergangs.

As he neared home, he went slower and slower. The thought of what might await him, made his feet grow heavier and heavier, and when he had separated from his last companion, he suddenly stopped and turned down by the chandler's, where the street led away from, and not towards his home.

It was now the third night Nikolai had been away, explained Mrs. Holman to the policeman outside; and it was not much wonder if he expected the reward he deserved, and felt his back smart. Lay hands on better people's children! And the son of Consul Veyergang, his own benefactor, too!

But where could he be? He could not possibly be in the timber-yard now, at this time of year.

His stronghold was not easy to hit upon either, for it was something very like looking in her own pocket. In common with other evil-doers, Nikolai was driven by an irresistible desire—like moths that flutter round a candle—to hide himself as near as possible to the place of his fear and dread, where Mrs. Holman was, and where he could catch a glimpse of Silla.

Holman lay at night and felt, through his intoxication, that things were going wrong with Nikolai. He heard it dripping and dripping in the thaw outside—splash, splash! The sound came in a monotonous chant : Ni-ko-lai, Ni-ko-lai.

He would ruin his health out there!

With sudden energy he sat up in bed. Where else would Nikolai be than under the old carriage hood that stood in the loft over the coach-house, mouldy and dropping to pieces with its opening towards the wall?

It was in the light of this idea that he rushed out.

Nikolai never felt the blockmaker's hand; he still slept on happily, as it lifted him up by the coat collar.

It was only when he stood erect on both feet that he grasped the situation, and threw himself down again, kicking and screaming. He would not go home, they might kill him first, or take off his head!

The heels of his boots made it evident both to sight and feeling that he meant it: he was utterly beside himself.

Only let Holman get him inside the door, and the strap should dance! Holman had worked himself up into a state of excitement.

Mrs. Holman was waiting in the doorway with a

candle. By its light she saw an ashy pale face, with
eyes staring at her, and at the same time heard the
words: "You won't get me in! If I was born in
the street, I can live in the street!" She caught a
glance from the sharp, defiant grey eyes—then out
of the blockmaker's hands, out of the gate, and he
was gone!

The blows on Ludvig's nose had gone to Barbara's
heart. But when she heard that Nikolai had run
away from the Holmans' and that there was some
talk of getting him into an institute for morally
depraved children, there was crying and weeping.
She had had shame enough with the boy, and this
she could not survive! Her mistress must prevent it.
She was conscious of having done her duty and
more than her duty all these years that she had been
Ludvig and Lizzie's nurse, but she could not put up
with this! Her mistress must prevent it, or she did
not know what she might do, or what might happen:
she felt quite capable of leaving them.

Barbara sat sighing and weeping in the nursery,
until the children were almost afraid to go in.

Such attacks generally lasted, at the most, one day;
but this one had now been going on for three, and
was disturbing the comfort of the house. Then Mrs.
Veyergang got one of her headaches, and was going
to have an afternoon nap, her accustomed cure,
during which everything must be kept perfectly
quiet around her.

It was Barbara who generally guarded her slumbers by going hushing and quieting right out into the kitchen, and keeping watch at the door into the passage. But now she only sat in her room sobbing.

It did surprise her a little that her mistress lay so quiet all the time without calling her. On the other hand, she rather enjoyed the sentence she was carrying out. Her mistress should know what opposing her meant, even if it were to last the whole week.

It grew dark, and still her mistress lay there. She lay until the Consul came driving home towards evening; and she did not even ring for lights when she got up.

It was with a shawl about her head and a face red with weeping, that Mrs. Veyergang received her husband that evening; she was in a violently excited state of mind, and her voice quite trembled.

She wanted nothing less than that he should give Barbara warning.

A tyranny existed in the house that was quite unparalleled—had existed for several years—and if she had put up with it without complaining— her husband knew that she had never complained —it was for the children's sake. But it was really unnecessary now, and "it may be just as well to seize the opportunity; she has become far, far too overbearing in the house!"

It was a matter of course that the warning was given in the most appreciative and considerate, although firmly decisive manner. The whole circle

of Mrs. Veyergang's acquaintance agreed that they
had all expected that the Veyergangs would really
one day part with that pampered creature!

The only person who was thoroughly astonished
and quite stunned, as if by a thunder-clap, was
Barbara herself; and for a long time she could not
understand that she, the Veyergangs' Barbara, had
actually received warning to leave Ludwig and Lizzie
and the house where she had been so indispensable.

She went about with a solemn, injured air, and
expected that a change of decision would some day
take place. Then she became humble to her mistress,
and wept before the children.

But there was always only the same kindness,
which ever clenched the dismissal more firmly.

And now her mistress began to talk about
a substantial acknowledgement of her services
with which the Consul would present her on
her departure

In indignation Barbara tied the strings of her best
bonnet beneath her chin, and with offended dignity
requested permission to go into town.

Her mistress was to know the meaning of this
when she returned later in the day. It was nothing
less than that it was her fixed, resolute purpose to
offer herself to others who would appreciate her better
than the Veyergangs did.

She directed her wrathful steps straight to Scheele,
the magistrate's house: they had four children, and
were looking for a nurse. They were the Consul's

most intimate friends, where she would only need to present herself, and they would jump at the opportunity. How often the magistrate's wife had praised her management, and talked condescendingly to her, when they had dined at the Veyergangs on Sundays! She had more than once thought Mrs. Veyergang fortunate in having such a treasure in the house, and sighed over her own inability to find just such another.

But—how unfortunate it was—Mrs. Scheele was extremely sorry—they had just engaged another nurse!

"Fancy!" exclaimed Mrs. Scheele, when her husband came down from his office, "there is a revolution at the Veyergangs', and that high and mighty Nurse Barbara has got her dismissal. She has been here and offered herself to us. I wouldn't have that pampered creature at any price!"

Barbara walked a long way that day and to the best houses. On a large sheet of paper, folded in three, she had the Consul-General's long and excellent testimonial to exhibit; moreover she was fully conscious of the extent to which she was known. But though she stood so large and erect and smart at the door, and comported herself so well, there was no one who could make any use of her!

And late in the evening, later than was needful, as she did not wish to show herself, she came home again, disappointed and weary.

It really seemed as if all the celebrity she had

acquired during all these years, all her fidelity, all
her prestige as nurse at the Veyergangs, was to
vanish at one stroke into thin air!

Deeply hurt as she was after her unlucky expedi-
tion, it was remarkable that no one in the house
asked her how she had got on—though there were
plenty of mischievous glances from her fellow-
servants, whose standing with their mistress had
depended for so many years upon her. And whenever she tried to broach the subject with Mrs. Veyergang, the latter always turned the conversation—
indeed, once she even dismissed the subject, saying
that Barbara must know that she never meddled
with such things.

But the kindness increased as the day of her
departure approached. Barbara began to perceive
how this screw of kindness, that turned so gently,
was screwing her farther and farther out of the
house. The Consul had Nikolai placed on trial as
apprentice in a smithy down by the crane, and from
Mrs. Veyergang she received one thing after another,
as remembrances. But when, one day, the Consul—
very thoughtfully—made her a present of one of his
old travelling trunks, she let her large, heavy person
sink down upon its lid, completely overwhelmed.
She could not bring herself to think, had never
believed, that the day would come when she must
part from her mistress and Ludvig and Lizzie—it
would kill her!

This was a direct appeal to the Consul himself,

but the answer was not exactly as Barbara wished. He patted her on the shoulder, saying:

"I'm glad, my dear Barbara, that you feel that you have been well off."

When she went into the Consul's office for a settlement and to receive her savings-bank book—the amount it contained was a hundred and fourteen specie-dollars, a result, the Consul said, with which she ought to be thoroughly satisfied, when she considered the great expense she had been put to with Nikolai—she declared her intention of resting for a time before she went out to service again, and had made arrangements to lodge with a farmer out in the country: she had now been toiling for others for fourteen years!

The last evening, which she had dreaded so, went more easily than she had expected. The Consul and his wife were invited to the Willocks' country-house in the afternoon with the children, so the farewell could only be a short one, before they got into the carriage.

She was left standing with the feeling of Lizzie's soft fur, which she had stroked, in her fingers.

CHAPTER IV

A STOLEN INTERVIEW

HOLMAN made his usual turn into Selvig's public-house every evening to brace himself for his return home. When the ale-bottle had been emptied, and a proper number of drams consumed, his at first hurried, restless look was stiffened into a dull, staring, fixed mask. It was the crust about his heart, far within the unconscious, degraded man, who enjoyed his daily hour of oblivion to that life-struggle which he had taken upon himself when he chose to unite his lot inseparably with that of his duty-breathing wife, that life-struggle in which he continually declared "pass," and turned aside. When he sat there silently staring over his glass, it was felt that he was brooding over something, possibly only the number of drams he had drunk, possibly his bill, possibly, too, a remote world of thought, where, like a philosopher, he gazed silently down into unfathomable depths. Or possibly he was musing in silent resignation upon the problem of matrimony, and the strange law of consequence which had set him down here in the public-house.

But regularity in all things, said Holman, and
when the clock struck eight, with his tools in his
hand and his head bent, he turned his faltering steps
homewards.

On Saturday evenings, when work was over at
the workshop, a tall, active young girl, with large
wrists, thin arms and a stooping figure, would often
come down to fetch him. She had a basket, and a
piece of paper on which was written what she was to
buy with the week's wages.

The two would then go up the street together,
walking slower and slower as they went. Time after
time he would stop, and look thoughtfully about him
with one hand in his pocket, and an occasionally
ejaculated "H'm, h'm!"—until they arrived at
Mrs. Selvig's steps and green door, when he would
suddenly declare that he had some "things" lying
in there: he would be out again directly.

Silla knew by experience what "directly" meant,
and meanwhile went her own way over the yards.

Through the lovely August evening, one troop of
workmen after another came over the bridge near the
mouth of the river, several of them with the same
sort of escort as her father, of wife or child. It
was so usual and its meaning so self-evident, that no
one ever gave it a thought.

While the different gates and yards were emitting
their streams of workmen, Silla had approached one
of the narrow passages with which the loading places
are furrowed. On each side was a wooden hoarding,

and there were stacks of timber within. The irregularly cut up, black muddy roadway led into a forge and implement yard.

Just at the corner lay a heap of rubbish, full of broken bottles and pottery. She stood there with her basket, every now and then taking a step backwards, up the heap, to make room for passers-by. In this way she gained the top of the heap, and could see over the hoarding into the yard.

They were still busy receiving wages in there in a crowd round a little shed which did duty as an office.

With outstretched neck, and her two shining dark eyes turned almost like a bird's, she stood and looked eagerly in. There was no mistake about her object.

"Well, lass! are you looking for your sweetheart?" said a voice below.

But, as she at that moment caught sight of Nikolai, and he signalled to her, she took no notice of the voice, and waved her basket vigorously.

He came out down the passage, unwashed and sooty, straight from his work.

"He's gone now!"

"Who?"

"He had red hair, and had on blue braces and a sailmaker's cap. I think it was the man from Grönlien they call Ottersnake; and he accused me of standing here and looking for my sweetheart!"

"I'll sweetheart him! If I only get hold of him,

I'll hammer him into nails! And then I'll pull his red hair to oakum, so that his father will only need to put it into the pitch-kettle!"

He looked about; but as the Ottersnake, who was doomed to so cruel and terrible a fate, was nowhere to be seen, his wrath suddenly subsided, and with an upward movement of the head, he proposed:

"Baker Ring's, Silla?"

He had his week's wages in his pocket, so they made a short cut through two or three muddy back yards, which had planks laid down across the worst places, up to the baker's shop.

Oh, how they bought, and how they did eat!

There were some specially delicious expensive cakes with jam inside. And it was the two collars, that he had thought of buying for himself next week, that they ate up!

With a great feeling of his own importance Nikolai related how he had now forged six large iron hooks with links to them; and she must not imagine that they wanted nothing but hammering— no, they had to be hammered out and beaten and bent at the right time! Down there they only made stakes and picks and tires; but he meant to be either a locksmith or a brazier.

This did not interest Silla very much; she wanted to hear about the picnic on Sunday, when he had gone to the woods with the journeymen. It must have been awfully jolly! And didn't they dance too?

"I should just think they did. Anders Berg is a capital fellow; he's going to set up for himself in Svelvig soon, and get married."

"And were the others engaged, too?"

"Pshaw!".

"Well?"

"Pooh!"

"What's the matter with you? Can't you tell me?"

"Why, it's nothing—only nonsense! There's not one of them that'll make a smith's wife—creatures that have larks now with one fellow and now with another?"

"And did you dance?"

"Oh, the 'prentices have only to run after beer; but when I'm a journeyman—but, Silla, the time—we must hurry!" he broke off suddenly.

"Oh, it's not late yet. One more nice one with jam—do go in and buy it! Oh, do, Nikolai!" she begged, and as he ran in to get what she wanted, she called after him:

"And some sweets to eat on the way home—some of those at four for a halfpenny."

"Can't you eat it as you go along, Silla?" he urged, when he came out again; "you must make haste! Just think if she heard at home that you had been with me."

"Pooh, there's no hurry," and she leaned against the wall, and regaled herself—"for you see." she mumbled, "father won't be out of Mrs. Selvig's yet a-while, and I'll say first of all that *that* has kept me: I can reckon at least half an hour for that. And then to mother I have the excuse that it's Saturday evening, and there were so many people in the shop that I could hardly get to the counter. And when I won't have any supper, you know, I'll only say I've got such a headache with standing and waiting in the shop: it was so stifling in there. I think mother's nose would be very fine, if she could guess that I had met you. Well, what are you looking so solemn about ?"

"She at home"—he never named her mother in any other fashion—"forces you into lies every single day; no one has a right to speak the truth but her !"

"Oh !" she tossed her head impatiently; she had heard this so often.

"She eats up all the honesty in the room by herself, you know, for it's quite impossible to act honestly by her, for very terror. She keeps discipline, and much or little, it's all the same. Any one who wants to speak the truth without using his fists to back it up will get thrashed as I did ! It doesn't matter for me; but when I think of you going home and making up all those lies again, and that you are so frightened, and haven't the strength to stand against them, Silla !"

She tried to laugh and make light of it; but her face fell sadly. She could not bear this

unpleasant subject, for she was obliged to tell lies,
however angry he might be.

And then she suddenly began to hurry.

"No, no, we must go home, Nikolai. I daren't
stand here any longer."

Nikolai was starting off, but stopped suddenly at
sight of Silla's dismayed countenance. She had
turned her pocket inside out, and stood holding it
while she gazed and searched on the ground round
her. Then, in feverish haste, she unfastened her
bodice, and searched there.

"The money! Oh, the money, Nikolai!" she
cried anxiously, and went on shaking her skirt
and looking about her, almost beside herself. "The
silver was wrapped up in the two dollar notes, just
as father gave them to me, and I put them into my
pocket at once."

"What *shall* I do, Nikolai?" She began to cry,
but all at once, with a sudden thought, she flew to the
basket. But it was not there.

They searched and searched.

Of course it must be at the corner by the
rubbish-heap, for she had stood there and waved
her basket. It would be lying among the broken
bottles.

The pale, thin rim of the autumn moon had risen
over the yards while they were searching there step
by step, Silla every now and then uttering a despon-
dent, monotonous "Suppose I don't find it!" and
Nikolai plunging his arm up to the elbow into

puddles in which the roll of money might have
fallen.

They had been by the bridge, they had searched
the rubbish-heap, they had looked up and down and
everywhere; it was not to be found.

It was beginning to be late, and Mrs. Holman was
waiting at home. She would be really waiting now.

Silla began to cry.

Nikolai had only asked her once or twice to be
quiet, and he would find the money. Now he suddenly
said :

" I should like to give you another good feed of
cakes to-day, and then throw myself into the sea
with you, Silla. It would be no lie that we lay
there."

Whether his proposition was meant seriously or
not, it did not gain a hearing with her. She sat
hopeless and despairing on a log while the big tears
ran down her cheeks.

The seventeen-year-old workshop apprentice stood
thoughtfully, with his flat cap pushed back over his
rough hair, blackened by the week's work. He was
gazing intently into an old rotten hole in the log.
The hole became more and more rotten, more and
more hollow, more and more empty while his busy
thoughts were trying to find an expedient. But none
came.

Fully aware of her fate, Silla rose, took her basket,
and started homewards with her eyes fixed on the
ground. She was going to the scaffold.

D

Nikolai accompanied her as far as he dared, reiterating in different ways: "Don't be afraid, Silla, they can't kill you!"

Something like a low wail said that she heard him.

When she disappeared round the corner, he made a short cut which only he and one or two old yard cats knew of; and from the hoarding at the bottom of the square he saw her go, with bent head and the same quiet step, without stopping, down the cellar stairs.

When it was dark, he stood outside the window and listened. He heard her still sobbing quietly, after the storm that had passed over her.

Mrs. Holman had examined and cross-examined, and at last extracted from Silla the confession that she had been with Nikolai. That she, Mrs. Holman's daughter, in spite of all prohibitions, sought the society of that misled prodigal, who had rewarded her with such ingratitude, was enough to bring her to her grave. And no one would persuade her either that Holman's hardly-earned week's wages could vanish like steam from a kettle. A half-starved apprentice-boy, walking beside a well-filled pocket—any one could understand what the result of that would be. Master Nikolai had only carefully and craftily watched his time, when he knew that Silla had her father's money in her pocket, to get it shuffled into his own.

Matters were not improved by Silla in her

obstinacy declaring that he had not so much as seen the money—as if Nikolai would take a farthing from *her* !

This last remark sealed his fate—there should be no concealment of his conduct on Mrs. Holman's part.

There was a commotion in the forge-yard, when the next day a police-officer came and arrested Nikolai. He was to be taken to the police-station for having defrauded a young girl on Saturday evening of the whole of her father's week's wages.

But when they were gone, Anders Berg swore, as he brought the sledge-hammer down on the anvil, that that Nikolai had never done. The others—Jan Peter, and Katrinus, and Bernt Johan Jakobsen and Petter Evensen—they thought nothing; but to bring the police into a respectable work-yard! He had better get work in some other place after this !

For the first moment Nikolai had only one sensation—the paralysing fear by which a first acquaintance with the police is always accompanied. The feeling that he had a good conscience did indeed leap up within him, but only to die away again immediately. He had so often had that, and it had always proved to be too thin a sheet of ice to stand upon in the hour of trial. That kind of self-esteem was a plant which had too often been trodden under Mrs. Holman's heel to be able to bloom now as a fragrant, full-blown flower within him.

The outcome of his reflections was a sudden twist and a violent jerk, by which he hoped to escape from his inconvenient companion, the sole result, however, being that he immediately had a constable at each arm.

When brought up for examination before the police superintendent, a dark, unwilling defiance glowed in his face, and the sharp glance—too sharp for a lad of his age—did not prepossess any one in his favour.

Silla? He had not been with any Silla on Saturday.

It would never occur to him to betray her, and it was only when he was confronted with her and her mother, and heard that she had confessed, that he admitted it.

Silla continued to maintain, in a voice choked with tears, that he had not taken the money, but this proved nothing either for or against him. On the other hand what had more weight were the facts that had been elucidated on ransacking and examining the room in which he lodged—he lived in a garret at glazier Olsen's with three other apprentices—for they all agreed in saying that on the Saturday in question he had come home late, after they were asleep, and had gone out again very early on the Sunday morning.

The assertion of the accused that this was to

renew the search for the lost money down by the yard did not seem very credible. But it was impossible to get any nearer to him.

A hardened young rascal. This was his foster-mother's testimony too.

Nikolai stood with his cap in his hand, looking down at the floor. He had a habit of drawing the skin of his forehead up and down when he was meditating. In the broad, young face with the large features, the grey eyes into which there sometimes came a peculiar look, and the cock's comb, of a tinge between zinc and copper, the police inspector's penetrating and—after many year's practice—not easily deceived eye saw the marks of one who would probably in the future often give occupation to the police.

" In order to exclude the possibility of conferences with the other apprentices in his room," he dictated for the record, " considering that the accused has manifested *mala fides* by an attempt to escape, as well as by his untruthful conduct and denials under examination, he will, for the present, be placed under arrest."

As the words of the order were read out, there were a few involuntary contractions of the muscles in Nikolai's face, which was damp with perspiration; there quivered in it the poor man's curse, at never having a way of escape; a false step, and he is caught, a lost dollar, and he comes before the court.

After another examination Nikolai was acquitted
for want of evidence.

The morning when the prison door closed behind
him, he slunk down the street with a feeling that all
the windows on both sides were looking at him; it
was anything but the gait of one who can let his
honesty's sun shine once more.

Down at his lodging at Mrs. Olsen's he found his
few things put ready in the cupboard under the
stairs to be fetched away, and a message was left
that his place in the garret was occupied by some
one else.

He did not ask why. Mrs. Olsen's silence hurt
him more than if she had cried aloud about people
who drew on her " an examination and search of the
house, and other disturbances."

And then he had to go down and show himself at
the forge again—to Hægberg the master, and Anders
Berg, and the journeymen, and all the apprentices.

It was with uncertain steps and stopping time
after time. What did Anders Berg think, he wondered.

In a fit of despondency he half turned. But he
must do it. So he held up his head and began to
whistle. But as he neared the coal-begrimed wooden
palings of the work-yard the whistling ceased, and
he was in a cold perspiration when he entered the
gate.

Without saying a word he went to the coal-bin
and began to lift some bars of pig-iron which had

to be moved aside. While he did so, no one either greeted or spoke to him.

Anders Berg had an iron in the furnace, and it was not until he and another man had finished hammering it out, that he came up to Nikolai and said :

" I was sure you would come back again. Here's some work for you ; you can file these three keys."

Whereupon Nikolai was placed at one of the vices, and was soon busily at work with both coarse and fine files.

Anders Berg's words had done him such good, had placed him at once as it were on his feet before the whole workshop, and in his heart he made a vow of friendship and devotion to Anders Berg for ever.

There were showers of sparks and a ringing from the sledge-hammers in the large smithy, and sharp blows of hammers, while the files shrieked and whistled and set one's teeth on edge. The work went on and Nikolai thought he had never known until to-day how splendid it was to be a smith. He might as well do the key-bit with the fine file at once, while the key was on that side of the vice ; and he filed the notch as neatly and smoothly as if it had been intended for a chest of drawers, and not a great pipeless key for a wooden gate.

Now came the handle. He worked away with the coarse file, until he could scarcely hear the sledge-hammer for its shrieking.

At the anvil stood a man making clincher nails,

while one of the apprentices pulled the bellows and occasionally gathered the nails together. They were talking and laughing, and now and again some loud exclamation penetrated to Nikolai. It was only when the boy made a grimace at him, that it occurred to Nikolai that he was the subject of the conversation, and instantly the large file became quite light in his hand, and he had suddenly eyes and ears only for what was going on around him.

They were standing talking and nodding over there by the vices; Jan Peter ran and repeated what this one said and what the other one said. It was easy to see what the meaning of it all was, and that he now stood there like any show animal; no, like something much worse—like one who was capable of going to the pockets of any one of them!

There was not one of the apprentices who would share his night's lodging with him now. He could see that.

He stood straining his ears, with a feeling that they were killing him in all the work-yards round— they were filing him down at the vices, hammering him flat with the small hammers, and crushing him with the sledge-hammers. He guessed and under-stood glances and looks.

"Well, you know, Matthias," he heard from away there by the nails which the man was now gathering into his apron, "there are many easier trades than standing in a smithy: make a good pick out of your fists, lad!"

"He-he-he!" laughed the boy addressed.

"Or make yourself pincers that you can get down into skirt-pockets with—all the lassies in the town, lad, that have any pence."

Nikolai heard every word and the hoarse laughter that followed; he was very pale.

Coarse merriment shone in the man's sooty face, and, as their eyes met, he made a contemptuous grimace.

Soon after he came past with his apron full of nails. Their eyes met again; the scornful ones grew more scornful; Nikolai seemed to see them in a haze, and then the journeyman received a blow full in the face which laid him on his back, scattering the nails as he fell.

There was a short pause of surprise before they all rushed upon him.

But Nikolai swung the big file about him like a madman. He felt with frenzied pleasure, how he would strike—strike down the whole smithy one by one until justice was done him. Wait a little, he had only begun yet—a hammer was lying on the block.

But the men in the smithy did not wait, and the next moment it was he who lay on his back, his eyes blinded by blue and yellow sparks, and as many of his adversaries around and upon him as there was room for; he should be held fast and sent about his business now—he had used a weapon!

He felt a powerful grasp on his coat collar, a grasp

that included the skin, felt himself dragged up and, without a pause, half carried, half flung, out of the smithy door.

It was Anders Berg, who had exerted his power to rescue him, and who—still only slightly relaxing his hold—led him out of the gate.

It was his farewell to the smithy.

"I'll just tell you something," exclaimed Anders Berg later, when the commotion had subsided; he was still red in the face and spoke loudly, while he hammered cold.

"There's come a wrong bend in Nikolai; but it isn't his fault!"

The hammer rang on the iron.

Nikolai did not take a lodging anywhere that evening; he was too bruised and dirty for that, his clothes too torn and ragged, and, more than anything else, he felt too sore to meet people now that he had left the smithy in such a way.

When night fell, he had once more taken up his familiar quarters in one of the stacks of planks down at the timber-yard. There, in one of the deep square spaces he lay and looked up at the stars and thought how entertaining the world had become!

CHAPTER V

AMONG THE UNEMPLOYED

NIKOLAI was out of work, that was very certain.

It never entered his head to present himself at any other smithy: they all knew each other too well for that. And even at barge-builder Hansen's, where he got a lodging up in the tool-loft, and his food on the days when he got a chance of doing something useful, they wanted to know now why he had left his trade. As if that were any business of theirs!

So Nikolai suddenly disappeared.

On the quay, the harbour and the steamers, a fellow with his hands could surely get on just as well as any other.

It was with fresh and dauntless courage, though with a stomach not overladen with food during the last few days, that he went down there.

He was received with a certain appreciative admiration. He found that it was a well-known fact that he had had an encounter with the police, and had been sufficiently dexterous to get off without their being able to fix anything upon him; the news of such an exploit travels like wild-fire in that world, and spreads a halo around its subject.

And as long as he was supposed to be only an idler, or an apprentice who was airing himself and taking a day or two's holiday from the smithy, the shareholders in the different businesses down there were both agreeable and talkative. But when—and that not once only—he suddenly turned to, and darted over the landing-stage from the steamer with a large trunk on his back and a traveller at his heels, past the cabs up to the hotel, they quite changed their tone. Had he a badge? Or did he think perhaps, that it would do to take other people's business? They knew very well what sort of a fellow he was!

He was well aware that he could not get a badge, so he must get along as he best could by working and toiling and fighting for an empty stomach, and make his way by threats and with his fists, and—when it was a case of being entrusted with a burden, or getting first hold of a trunk—by being deaf, stone-deaf, to everything they might think of calling out about him.

There were ten men to every job requiring one, and, as it were, a wall or circle drawn round every road to earning something. Some small jobs he might now and then chance to be alone in—when the lock of a door had slipped, or the door came off its hinges, or some kind of smithcraft was required at a moment's notice. But he gained no more than a bare subsistence, often only a dram or two by way of thanks.

And now that it had been such a long winter, he was both hungry and cold. The nights especially were so long. He often took spirits for his supper to get them to pass. And then he had to think over what he would try his hand at the next day— cutting the ice, work on the quay, clearing away snow or carrying planks in the yard.

Thinly-clad and with no overcoat, and rather red with the cold, he clattered down in a coat that was in holes at the elbows, and his old scarf that had taken its hue from the smithy, pulled high up about his ears. It was not difficult to see in him the smith's apprentice. Whenever he met any of Hægberg's men, he burst into a scornful laugh. Did they think, perhaps, that he was slovenly clad? It was just as he was now, that he wanted to be. He wanted to be free and have neither master nor journeyman nor any one over him, and to care for nobody.

If the forge-yard was one point that he preferred to keep away from, there were also other places in the town that he made a round to avoid—namely, that part of the quay where the blockmaker's workshop lay, and the Holmans' house up in the square.

Whatever the reason might be, he had no wish to meet Silla.

The last time he had spoken to her—the day

after he had left the smithy—he noticed that she
was looking about in a frightened way the whole
time, and wanted him to stand first in one place and
then in another.   It could not be fear of any one
at home, and then it suddenly dawned upon him
that she was ashamed that people should see her
standing and talking to him, so with a " Good-bye,
Silla ! " he darted from her.

Afterwards he thoroughly enjoyed seeing her
look so unhappy and so eager to show him that
she did not care what people thought.   What did
she care about him, when he had nothing to treat
her with ?   It was not fit for her to stand talking to
a fellow like him.

There is a splendid friend and ally for every one
who has thin, ragged clothes, and that is the sun.
He distributes overcoats in the shape of warm,
sunny walls, brings life and movement with him,
and then there need no longer be any uncertainty
about a midday-meal.

Nikolai had had work on the quay the whole
morning, and was now standing, in the midday rest,
baking himself against the sunny wall, and yawning.

He stopped in the middle of a yawn.   That
slight figure in the faded cotton dress, that was
running with her body bent forwards, and a handkerchief over the little, dark head, to keep off the
sun—it was no other than Silla !

She was darting along among the baskets and
traffic on the fish-quay; there was a searching haste

in her like that of a frightened corn-crake, that
turns its head now to one side now to the other
as it runs. She had caught sight of him, and now
she began calling :

"Nikolai! Nikolai!

"Nikolai!"—she almost choked in her hurry to
speak—"Nikolai, just think! Mother, when she
was unpicking my old blue dress to-day, she found
the money in the lining, inside the lining, both the
notes, and the silver too. I ran down to tell you
directly I had taken father's dinner to the workshop.
And now I'm going to the smithy, and they shall
hear what they have done to you. Could you
believe it! Inside the lining! I am so awfully,
awfully glad "—and her eyes did look almost wild—
" You can't think what a grave face mother put on!"

" Just tell them at home that it's all the same to
me!" said he bitterly and unmelted. But she did
not notice it; she wanted to go to the smithy, and
away she went.

He had no objection. But now that Anders Berg
had set up for himself in Svelvig, there was no one
there he cared about, to hear it. For he was a free
man now !

He stood with his hands in his trouser pockets,
gazing over the edge of the quay at a sunken sugar-
loaf, which a crowd of small boys, amid noise and
clamour, were labouring to get up. It lay already
half melted on the green bottom, on which the sun
drew wavy lines.

Silla might try all she could to get him into the smithy. Since they had tacked the word thief on to him, he had got soaked through with salt water, just like the sugar-loaf. And besides, to stand there and slave, when he could be his own——

"Hi, you boys! I'll show you how to get the sugar-loaf up, but you will have to eat it yourselves."

*　　　*　　　*　　　*

The public-house—the one at Mrs. Selvig's, with the green door and white window frames, farthest down the street—had seen Holman's quiet, subdued, stooping figure come and go for many years. His grasp on the door-handle was just as precise, his walk up to the brown counter after having laid down his tools, exactly the same, though his face had a little more colour in it. He had a certain reputation there, which had allowed of his "chalking up" for several years past, and there was a regular proportion of his account, about which his inexorably correct wife had not the faintest idea—"for Holman had his weekly pocket-money."

And as usual on Saturday evenings, Silla was walking about outside with the basket, waiting for him.

She was really quite nicely dressed in her cotton gown with a little white handkerchief tied round her neck; but clothes did not seem to set her off. The slight, overgrown figure seemed to show through everywhere.

She made a quick turn, when she thought she caught a glimpse of Nikolai at the bottom of the street. She had fancied the same thing last Saturday evening. She had not really spoken to him since early in the summer, when he got so angry because she wanted him to go into the smithy again.

She went quickly down the street—she was quite certain that it was he!

She hurried on farther, down to the bridge; but it was the same as last time—he was not to be seen. So she turned back again, disappointed, keeping constant watch on Mrs. Selvig's green door. She knew her father would appear as the clock struck eight.

She went up towards it and down again: she began to grow impatient. It must be past the time. They were beginning to shut the shops here and there, and if she was to get anything bought this evening, it would be impossible to wait any longer.

She must really go up and see whether her father were sitting there still—whether he had not perhaps gone when she was down at the bridge: he never mistook the time.

She had gone up the street as far as the place where the stone pavement began, when she saw the green door open and slam quickly to again, as a bare-headed, half-dressed servant-girl ran out. Immediately after, a man came out in similar haste, and through the door which he left standing open

E

behind him, a number of people, with and without hats, streamed out on to the steps.

Something was the matter!

Now a window was also opened, or rather hammered open, so that the pane clashed down on to the pavement.

Probably some drunken man or other, who could not stand any longer—it was Saturday evening, you know—and who was making a row, and must be taken by the police.

She had often seen such sights before, and was quite accustomed to them. She was not anxious about her father either: he never interfered in such matters.

But why did he not come out? Every one else had come out.

A faint, slanting gleam of evening light had fallen in through the empty square of window. Her father generally sat at the table just inside; he always kept the same place. And she went up and peered in between the flower-pots,—some half-stifled, dirty geraniums and hydrangeas, saturated with public-house effluvia.

Who was that—that man who was lying on the dirty counter, with his necktie and shirt unfastened and one arm hanging down—was it her father?

"If only some one had a lancet!—he moved just now—a lancet!"

What more they said on the steps she did not notice, except that some wanted to deny her entrance, and others again said that she was Holman's daughter.

She awoke, as if after a fall from a great height during which she had lost consciousness, to find herself sitting by the counter supporting her father's head. She thought she remembered clinging to his neck and begging him to answer her: but there was no rattling in his throat now.

They had placed an old, worn sofa-pillow and the seat of a chair under his head. Behind stood quart and pint measures, dram-glasses, tin funnels and beer-bottles pushed right up to the wall to make room. His wide-open eyes stared up at the once white-washed beams of the ceiling, and one side of his face was drawn up into a grin, which made him look as if he were unspeakably disgusted with the dirty ceiling.

A big man sat at the door. Silla knew him: he was the public-house bear, as he was called; he who turned people out for Mrs. Selvig. He was sitting silent on the bench.

There was perfect stillness in the room; she heard only the drip from the tap of the brandy-cask down into the dish beneath, and saw, through the half-open door to the inner room, Mrs. Selvig and her two daughters bustling about on tiptoe.

A young man in spectacles entered. He asked a few rapid questions, while he opened a case of instruments on the counter at the feet of the prostrate figure. He listened at its chest with the stethoscope and without it, and shook his head, pulled out a lancet, and pushed the shirt sleeve up the hanging arm.

"Hold the sleeve, so that it doesn't slip down!" he said with a glance up at Silla; he took her to be a member of the household.

The lancet pierced and pierced again. The ashen grey face of the girl looked into his, as if she would beg him for only one drop of that which was the life.

There came out something like a thick, dark syrup.

He listened again, felt again; one more trial with the lancet, and it was with an air of superiority, and a mouth drawn up like his professor's, that the young bachelor of medicine turned to those assembled and pronounced his concise verdict:

"Stone dead! The man's stone dead!—from drink!"

His words were followed by a cry from Silla, who threw herself upon her father.

"Is that his daughter?" asked the young doctor. He carefully wiped his lancet at the light, and put his instruments together preparatory to going, but gazed at the same time over his spectacles at her. Heedless of everything, she cried incessantly over the body.

"You aren't dead, are you, father? Father!"

It was a wild sorrow, without consideration or bashfulness, and the young doctor felt that he was witnessing an unpleasant scene from life in the outskirts of the town. He had done his duty and hastened out.

A twenty-year-old workshop apprentice, pale and overcome, was standing behind Silla, trying to recall her to herself. He took her by the shoulder, and whispered repeatedly, as loudly as respect for the dead would allow:

"Silla! Silla! don't you hear? It's me— Nikolai!"

And he tried in vain two or three times to lift her up from the body.

Meanwhile a policeman stood and examined Mrs. Selvig and the girls. He made notes, and took down the particulars of the death.

Just finished his usual quantity, a bottle of ale and four drams. The girl at the bar saw him quickly stretch out his hand—had the impression that he wanted another dram—and when he slowly sank down from his chair, supposed that he was drunk. Used never to be so drunk that he could not walk or stand, at any rate by supporting himself or holding on to convenient, firm things.

This last piece of evidence was deposed to by several of the regular customers, or as they were described in the police report — "Several of the regular visitors to the refreshment-room, whose testimony may be considered as thoroughly reliable."

Several of these silent, somewhat tottering, figures

who had been thus aroused from their dull, Saturday evening drowsiness, had already disappeared from the scene. Bottles and glasses remained standing with their contents.

"Might there not possibly be some other direct or indirect cause ?"

It was at first hesitatingly that Mrs. Selvig could think of anything of the sort.

Unwilling as she was to go to extremes with an old, regular customer, she yet had been obliged this evening to give him to understand that whatever he required in future must be paid for in cash. His bill had now, after all the years he had enjoyed credit in the tap-room, grown so enormous, that she, a widow with two daughters, could no longer feel justified in letting it run on. During all the years he had frequented her house, she had faithfully kept her word never to send a bill home to his house. But a bill cannot lie for ever on the threshold, as the police know. That is the way of the world : it is the same for one as it is for the other—so it must just be got by a distress warrant. That was what she had said to him, unwilling though she had been to do so, and so unpleasant, she could truthfully say, as it was to disturb such a quiet, decent man.

It was high time to rid the bar of its encumbrance. The public-house bear had hunted up a hand-barrow, but had to get a couple more men to help carry. And they must have a proper contrivance with a cloth

over, so that the whole thing would look like a
hospital stretcher—a dead man with nothing but
a tablecloth over him would make too great a commotion out in the street!

It was something of this kind that Mrs. Selvig
and her daughters were busy looking out and
putting together, out of some green bed-hangings.
One's good name is dear to every one, and Mrs.
Selvig felt that what had just taken place was a
blow to the house.

It was now nearly dark in the tap-room. Holman's
dark figure had been moved on to the stretcher,
which stood on the floor ready to be lifted, and a
message had been sent to Mrs. Holman.

Perhaps they delayed purposely; a little later in
the evening when it was darker, and an undesirable
sensation in the street would be avoided.

Silla's face was stiff with crying. There was no
one in the room but her and Nikolai.

He stood by the counter, and she was sitting with
her back to the window; there was no sound but
the humming of a gnat in the half-darkness up
under the curtain.

At last he broke the silence.

"He was kind, both to you and to me, as often
as he dared be, you know."

Silla did not answer.

"He always dreaded going home at night so, you
know. He'll be spared that now, and setting his
foot inside this public-house again, too!"

"Father! Father!" broke from Silla, followed by a fit of violent sobbing.

"Listen, Silla!" he said, interrupted by the repressed weight on his own breast. "If you have no father, you have some one here who will take care of you, and knows what it is—I have never had any father either, nor ever seen any. And I *will* be a smith, as there won't be any more block-making for you now. I only wanted to tell you, so that you can remember it afterwards," he added softly—it did not look as if Silla were listening to him.

"And this evening I'll follow you right to the corner, and I'll stand there until everything is in, and I shall be outside to-night; so you know it, if anything is wanted."

"Yes, stay outside, Nikolai!" she whispered.

The public-house bear and the two bearers came in. They lifted the stretcher out through the door, and, with a little difficulty at the turn, down the steps, where a few spectators stood.

And so they went up the street—the dead with the two bearers and the public-house bear in front, and Silla and Nikolai behind.

At the place where they were to part, he pressed the basket, which she had forgotten, into her hand, and then stood looking after them.

CHAPTER VI

THE FACTORY GIRLS

WHAT becomes of all the swarm of orphan children down in the by-streets and outskirt alleys of the capital—children of whom no one has any account, and no one takes any account, who swarm down there only one floor higher, so to speak, than the spawn and small fry which are floating below in the sea among the quay piles, and which will one day become large male and female fish?

Disease wields a broad broom in the earliest age. The harbour takes them into its embrace; the streets with their stray livelihoods, or a wandering vagabond life, takes them; refuges, police-stations, prisons and the house of correction take them. In later years, labour also, on a great scale, has taken them into its embrace—the factory doors stand wide open.

People who now and then have an attack of conscientious scruples about existences to which they may possibly stand in original relationship, can draw a sigh of relief. The responsibility is at any rate diminished, as the chances now are that they

will be drawn into Labour's educating wheel; and
then, too, the matter is in certain respects carried
over into moral territory.

There they sat, the more ripely-developed youth
of the town, in rows up in the rooms of the Veyergang firm's great factory, and minded the whirring
shuttles, balls and rollers—Swedish Lena, and Stina,
and Kristofa, and Kalla, and Josefa and Gunda, and
all the rest of them. Had any one asked them about
their parents, they would now and then have been
hard put to it for an answer.

The conversation went on very busily at the top
of the room; it was even continued with nods and
glances whenever one or other of the controlling
authorities turned his steps in that direction. They
had to gesticulate, nod, talk in a loud voice, but
they got on best with their faces close up to one
another in all this whizzing, where the band-wheels
each whirred away for their little sub-division of
power, the boards of the floor quivered and shook
with the movement of the engines, and the waterfall
outside in the sun, with a thundering and deafening
roar, buried the great water-wheel beneath its
creamy, powerful splendour.

They were for the most part quite young vagabond girls of from barely sixteen to twenty, who
were making the noise up there : new-comers, more
or less, without practice, who were still striving to
acquire the knack. And that was Silla Holman,
she with the dark hair, slender and freckled, with

heelless slippers and a large spot of paraffine on
the front of her dress, who coughed and questioned,
and questioned and coughed, while her eyes looked
like two little round, black fire-balls, and her weak,
flat chest went up and down with the mere exertion
of making herself heard. She sat there among the
youngest; her fingers worked among the spools, and
now and then she looked up like a bird.

They had got over the angry dispute about
Josefa's new braided jacket. She need not try
to persuade any one that she had got the money
from her stepmother; no, let any one who liked
believe that, but neither Gunda nor Jakobina did!
Then Kristofa had related her wonderful adven-
ture of last Sunday—she was always passing through
remarkable occurrences, most wonderfully interesting, if not true to quite a corresponding degree, in
which fine ladies and gentlemen played the principal
parts, and she chanced to be the initiated one.

And now the conversation had turned upon
something so interesting that Silla listened with
both her ears. There was to be dancing on
Sunday evening up at the Letvindt, and the talk
was of handkerchiefs, bows, and finery—which
some possessed and others had to borrow—and of
who danced best and treated most liberally. Kristofa was able to inform them that there was to
be a violin and a clarionet, and that both students
and ordinary people and ships' officers were to be
there!

Some strangers who were going over the factory came up the room, and stopped and questioned and examined. And the young workwomen sat each in her place, with head bent over her work, as if she had no thought for anything but her reels.

The morning light shone with a kind of dizzy stillness in from the great windows high up in the wall, over human beings, machinery and bales.

It was nearly twelve. The last hour always dragged so slowly, and the smell of oil and the heat from the engines seemed to increase and become almost stupifying.

Still a few more long stifling minutes. At last the bell rang.

And dressed, as if by a stroke of magic, the factory girls swarmed down the steps, with their breakfast-tins in their hands, in their neat aprons, handkerchiefs nicely tied under their chins, and knitted shawls crossed over their chests.

Oh, the bright spring air!—to take a good breath of it! Silla, hot and thirsty, knocked off a bit of frozen snow from the fence with her tin and ate it.

With her head full of all that Kristofa had held out to her about the dance at the Letvindt, she wandered down arm-in-arm with a long row of her companions. The road out from the factory was quite crowded ; lower down it widened out, with a street-like pavement.

"Look, look, Kristofa! Veyergang has come back from England already!" The young girls nudged each other, highly interested. "New top-coat; light, light brown!"

"Pooh! *I* saw him come by the steamer yes-terday, him and a whole heap of English people. They were all brown together; I counted exactly seven different kinds of dirt-colour!" It was Josefa who was using her tongue; she had had practice at a milliner's.

"He'll have to take care of the oil!" tittered one.

"He's awfully handsome! Look what a grand forehead! Oh, what a lovely red silk handker-chief in his breast-pocket!" whispered Kristofa to Silla.

The row squeezed themselves up against the fence. The person in question came by humming carelessly, with his head held high and swinging his walking-stick. All the young girls stared respectfully and stupidly straight in front of them, though not without a glance out of the corner of their eye. He disappeared up the stream, cleaving it like a salmon.

"He parts his hair at the back of his head!"—"His hat is like a pudding-basin!"—"Don't breathe upon him, he is so thin!"—"He is his own father's son!"—"Oh, what a conceited stick!"

They had turned to look after him.

"He isn't nearly so stern as he walks there; but in the factory, you know, he has to be as firm as a rock. Johanna Sjöberg, who does clear starching, recognised him down at the masked ball at the fair; she told me so herself."

"You can just fancy," struck in Jakobina, "what a number of fine people come to the rooms in that way. You think you are only waltzing with a common man, and perhaps it is the son of the richest man in the town! But if you are a little careful you can easily tell by the way they dance, or by their watch, or their shirt-collar, or because they chew such fine tobacco."

"He looked at us, did you notice?" whispered Kristofa eagerly into Silla's ear.

"Yes, because he knows me," said Silla, a little confused at his having fixed his eyes on her.

There was a burst of laughter.

"Is that young crow going to caw too?"

The young crow grew hot beneath her handkerchief, but she did not answer. She knew quite well, that he did know her; he had been in the office when she went out with her mother to the Consul-General's to apply for a place in the factory.

A stream of girls from another factory fell like a tributary into theirs, and then through ramifications of streets and lanes, the whole flowed out into the irregular part of the town that was built of wood, below—through narrow entrances and up narrow flights of steps, into brown, red, white or grey houses, houses with slate roofs, with turf roofs, with tile roofs, and new houses that had barely been roofed.

Silla slipped into a narrow, damp entry. The sun shone through the cracks in the rotten woodwork full of bent rusty nails, and from time to time a dirty stream issued from beneath the gate, and disappeared into the gutter.

She stopped a moment as she heard her mother's righteous indignation venting itself within, in the familiar, dry, measured tones; and it was hesitatingly and with a depressed look that she opened the gate, behind which stood Mrs. Andersen's servant-maid, furiously red, and incapable of defending herself, while Mrs. Holman, her skirts fastened up, and her feet astride over the gutter-board, was rinsing and wringing out clothes. She was working calmly and deliberately; nothing in her cold grey eyes betrayed agitation.

" Mrs. Andersen ought at least to have the good sense to understand that clothes that had been used so long couldn't be got ready in one week. For that matter, you're welcome to tell her so from me. And I haven't been accustomed either, even in my humble position, to send clothes to the wash not patched or mended; and I can tell you that both Mother Nilsen next door and the people in this house have wondered to see the things that a person, who calls herself a chandler's wife, lets her husband and children wear ! No, you needn't contradict me, my good girl; when I say a thing, it's the truth.

And the stockings—we'll say nothing about them; for one heel was gathered up with a piece of twine, so that it was a disgrace to stand and wash them. People may look as high and mighty as they like—the wash speaks out!"

With slow, crushing significance she turned to her daughter.

"If you had come a little sooner, Silla, you might have saved me a great deal of work. But it's of no consequence; the sooner I'm dead and gone, the better. I've never wanted to live either, since your father went away."

"I'll help you wring, mother."

"Now it's all done? Many thanks! But it would have shown a little forethought, if you, who have only been sitting up in the factory, had hurried yourself a little to help your mother, who's had to stand and work hard all the morning."

"Thanks for the information, Mrs. Holman." It was Mrs. Andersen's servant, who had at last recovered her voice. "But I think you won't need to trouble yourself any more about our washing. It's much too plain and humble for such grand sentiments."

She dropped a curtsey, and then added, as she vanished quickly out of the gate:

"If only your soap-lye was half as sharp as your tongue!"

It was always Mrs. Holman's strong point, and one on which she prided herself, that she was always hungering and thirsting after righteousness in this world—in others. Inasmuch as part of this sentence also points inwards towards one's self, she was fortunate in finding her own doorstep well swept. She was also in the favourable position of being able to lay down both the law and the exceptions.

To every one comes a time when he is surrounded by a lustre, and that blockmaker Holman had existed was something which was really properly understood—perhaps by his wife too—only after he had disappeared from the scene.

The fact is, that it makes a great difference to a household whether it has the husband's work and weekly wages to subsist upon or not, and as a further aggravation of the situation, her dead husband's bill at Mrs. Selvig's thrust its extremely unexpected, unwelcome face into Mrs. Holman's room. Mrs. Holman could never get into her head that that bill was correct—why, Holman had had his fixed, regular pocket-money!

Mrs. Holman's bitter observations were numerous when she found herself compelled to choose between want and seeking work.

She had known to a pin's point how she would employ her husband's earnings in her own room, and occupied herself also with the way in which others might have things in theirs. During all these years, she had, so to speak, sat comfortably on the top of the load and driven; but now,

unfortunately, the day had come when she herself
must get down and draw—and that she felt herself
less fitted for.

It was when brought into this critical situation
that Mrs. Holman thought that if an exertion was
ever to be made, it must be made now—by whom,
she left unsaid. To this end she availed herself of
her acquaintance with Consul Veyergang to get her
daughter Silla taken into his factory. Unemployed
hands must have something to do, and it would, at
any rate, yield some small compensation for the
weekly money lost with her husband. If she then
stayed at home and kept house well, and in addition
mended and took in washing when it came in her
way, no one would venture to charge Mrs. Holman
with not knowing how to do her duty during these
hard days.

And she still discharged this duty of hers by strictly
keeping Silla from passing her leisure time in idleness, which was dangerous for young people. Sewing
and darning and patching all the evening—there
could be no better way of being trained in steadi-
ness.

But it was just while Silla sat and sewed and
darned and patched in the evening by the low oil-
lamp that the dancing and gaiety were best carried
on in her head, and that all Kristofa's and her
friends' word-pictures transformed themselves into
actual experiences. Bubble after bubble, the one

more wonderful than the other, floated up or burst right in front of Mrs. Holman's nose, while she sat knitting. She saw nothing, only wondered a little sometimes what there could be to smile and laugh at in the heel of a stocking.

CHAPTER VII

"THE WORLD IS RIGHT ENOUGH AFTER ALL"

Down in Hægberg's smithy it looked as if it were going to be not only blue Monday,* but blank Tuesday too. With the exception of one solitary figure, it was black and empty. Outside the door a row of iron picks, spades and crowbars, were waiting to be sharpened for the navvies on the new harbour works.

Hægberg was going about with his leather apron hanging down over one shoulder, as furious as a Berserk. There were no respectable men and apprentices to be had nowadays; but he would give them notice man by man, as sure as his name was Hægberg!

One was standing there grinding. And he had stood there quite alone, filing with all his might at his journeyman's probation work, the whole of St. John's day yesterday. That's how it is: one goes on the spree, and another pinches and is so stingy about

---

* An extra day's holiday taken by workmen after the lawful bank holiday is called "blue Monday"; if still another follows, it is called "blank Tuesday."

his money, that he would willingly lay his soul in
the fire for it.   The fellow was a good enough workman, to be sure, and if he had not had that affair
with the police, then—yes, no—no, yes, to be sure,
he was acquitted of that, so he was!

The person in question was Nikolai, who had
entered Hægberg's smithy again to complete his
years of apprenticeship.

Ah, at last! There came two men sauntering
over the yard to the smithy.

Hægberg turned round and pretended not to see
them; on consideration, it was not the time to part
with one's men.   He only went up himself and took
one of the crowbars out of the forge; and when the
two culprits arrived, he stood there, tall, lean, strong,
and grey-haired, hammering so that the sparks
flew.

This piece of work, unworthy of the master, spoke
louder than the angriest reproaches, and when in
silence he flung the crowbar down, and began
sharpening a pick, it was sufficiently evident that
there was thunder in the air.

By degrees during the morning they arrived, with
staring eyes, beating temples, and faces either pale
or red from being up all night, one with a swollen
eye, another with a plaster across his nose.   Their
voices were hoarse, and they each went silently to
work.   They must exert themselves if they were
to get through all the tool-work that remained.

Work went on uninterruptedly almost the whole

afternoon, without a word being spoken over the whole smithy. By that time most of the work had been got through, and Hægberg himself went out to do business in the town.

Those who were left at work shone with perspiration, and either because work had been the best cure for the excesses of the preceding Midsummer Day and Midsummer Eve, or it was the general relief at the departure of the master, one man began suddenly to sing, a couple more to yawn and stretch themselves lazily in the enjoyment of their pleasant recollections; and then the talk began about the way they had each spent their holiday.

Only Nikolai went on undisturbed; he cared more about a screw-hole in the hinge on his probation work than all their Midsummer Eve outings, and if he only worked away now, it would be finished by the end of the month.

His small hammer sounded above their talk,— the tar-barrels, wood-stacks and old house-walls that they had burnt, and their drinking and merriment until they had not a penny left,—haw-haw!

The hammer rang above it all.

Jan Petter had gone in a boat over to the islands, and seen so many bonfires,* both there and on the hills round, that it was impossible to count them.

* It is the custom in Norway on Midsummer Eve to burn large bonfires, which can be seen for many miles round.

Yes, when a fellow's drunk!

The hammer went on again.

One man stretched himself and yawned with the whole Midsummer holiday in his jaws. "Up on Grefsen ridge, cold punch had flowed down the hill as good as free. Veyergang's son had given the girls at the factory an old boat from Maridal Lake and half a barrel of pitch; heard the cuckoo and had larks all night—came down again when it was nearly eight o'clock."

The hammer rang no longer.

"Veyergang's son—the girls at Veyergang's factory!" Nikolai stood, anxious and uncertain, listening, and now and again glancing quickly and sharply over at the man who was speaking.

Then he washed off the soot, and disappeared.

* * * *

Silla had been down to the Valsets' cottage to fetch the customary evening pint of milk, when at the gate she met Nikolai. He said he had seen her go in, but she knew quite well that he had been watching for her.

"You can't think what fun I had on Midsummer Eve, Nikolai!" she said, holding out the can by the handle towards him. "If you only knew! No, never in all my life!"

"Up on Grefsen ridge?"

"How did you know; tell me, how did you know?"

"Oh, I—one of the smiths was up there. But

I can't understand how you could get away from her at home."

"No, it was a near chance, too, I can tell you!" She looked round, and said in a cautious whisper: "Mother doesn't know but that I lay and turned over in my bed at home all Midsummer night. She went to eat St. John's porridge with aunt out at Asker, and I was to stay at home, and iron; but at nine o'clock, I said good-bye and went my way. Oh Nikolai!"—she clapped her hands, laughing—"you should have heard how she scolded yesterday morning when she came back, because I was still in bed! Did you hear that we were treated to punch, too?"

"Who gave it you?"

"Ah, wouldn't you like to know! But, Nikolai, you won't tell. It was a certain person who treated us."

"Indeed!"

"He came up to see that they did not light the bonfire too near the wood. Yes, you must know, Nikolai, that it was no less a person than young Veyergang! There was a Midsummer party at his father's, and they were to see the fire from the stairs at exactly half-past eleven.

"And then he treated them to punch? You too?"

"It was just me! 'Her with the black eyes,' he said."

"Perhaps he has spoken to you before, too?"

" Yes, indeed ; he knows perfectly well that my name is Silla. I meet him every single day, you must know."

Nikolai made a movement as if he were bringing down a hammer on the hillside. " Indeed ! "

" Last Saturday in the office, when he had reckoned a *krone* too much in the pass-book, he said I could keep it and spend it on cakes."

" Ha ! ha ! Did he say that ? Wonderful, how kind he is ! " Nikolai said this with something that was meant for laughter. " The cook is very kind, too, when she feeds the goose so as to get hold of it ! "

He stood with one arm round the gate-post, looking at her; she had grown so pretty and elegant, and almost taller since he had seen her last. " A young girl who doesn't even know that she is pretty."

Silla pouted ; her whole expression was one of supercilious disavowal.

" If they offer her a cake, or a handkerchief, or a little fun, she stretches out her neck and runs up. I should think you might understand that, Silla, from all you see round you ! How many of them, I should like to know, will ever come to be the wife of an honest working-man ? They manage to dance a few times, and then it's all over. And they wanted to be just as kind to you now, Silla ! That Veyergang is on the watch for you ! If I'm not on the watch for him——" He suddenly looked pale and ugly.

"What are you thinking of, Nikolai? Don't go on like that!"

"You may well say what was I thinking of, to stand there grinding and filing away the whole month at my probation work, and then let you go up there among that pack of wolves. But I was born like that—that everything should go wrong with me!"

Silla stood, as she always did when Nikolai put on this tone, downcast and dispirited, her slender figure bending forwards, and her eyes on the ground.

"We two, Silla," he continued at length, with a shake as if of resolution, but his voice trembled—"we two have been, as it were, brought up together. And with things as they were, if they could make me go wrong, it would have been still easier for you to be twisted by them, for I was strong, you see; but you were weak, and had always to creep like a cat among lies and difficulties. And so—so—I thought that we two—who have always stood by one another—and I haven't had anyone else I could trust, as you know, Silla, and neither have you—that we should join hands. And if you're of the same mind, then——"

He had clasped his broad hands round the gate-post, and was squeezing it with all the strength of his square-set figure, while he waited for her answer. He gazed at her bent head, but she did not look up; and he drew a deep breath, for he felt that he must go on.

" And now I've got together a little money, and
not bought anything, and have filed and filed away
at my probation work; because when I become
journeyman, and another year has passed, and I've
laid by a little, then—then it might be that you
could get away from the factory dirt and the ordering
at home both at once, and be a real smith's wife,
Silla. You've never had any one to take care of you
as I've done, you know; and you don't know how
good I'll be to you! For a fellow who hasn't had
either father or mother, and since I was up at the
police-station I haven't had many companions
either——" But here his emotion overpowered
him.

" Such an uncommonly pretty smith's wife you
would make, Silla! If any one has eyes for a smith,
it's you; they are like sparks in the fire! And then to
come home and see only the top of your pretty little
black head at the room door! In spite of having
always been treated like a dog, and worse than that
—like a thief, it would all be nothing at all, if that
was how it could end. One's own room with a lock
on the door and the chest, that would be something
better than being dragged round a dancing-hall,
Silla, by fine fellows and sailors."

The last words, which were uttered in warm excitement, would have been better left unsaid; for,
from standing melted and overcome, with tears in
her eyes, she suddenly fired up against the
accusation.

"Do you want to deny me a little pleasure, too, Nikolai? I'm not to see any one, not to go anywhere. Oh no! I'm to be a girl who has never danced, a regular queer bird, that's first been kept in a cage by her mother, and then by——" her voice quivered, and she began to cry. "Is that what you call being kind to me, Nikolai? You must be trying to make me afraid of you, too!"

"Afraid of me?—of me, Silla?"

"Don't they all look upon me as a baby that's tied to her mother's apron-strings? And now you come and want to help her, Nikolai. That's right! That's right! Only keep me in! Oh yes, you and mother! It's only a question of who gets the power over me. But you'd better take care, Nikolai!"

She began to cry bitterly in impotent rage.

"Oh, well, cry away! I won't say anything. You've got some one else to comfort you for a little while," he added moodily.

She suddenly sprang up, went up to him, and laid her arm confidingly on his shoulder.

"Don't you *know* that I'll be your wife, Nikolai?" she said, looking full and ardently into his eyes; there were still tears on her dark, freckled face.

"Well, if you will, Silla, you shall see who can work."

"But mother, Nikolai! Oh, I'm so frightened— so frightened only that she'll get to know that we sometimes meet. She looks at me so hard every time I've been an errand, and I've always been gone

so long. But when I sit darning and patching of
an evening, I sometimes imagine that you come in
so fine and rich, and that you own the whole of
Hægberg's smithy, so that mother has to give in."

"No, do you think about that, Silla? Then I
will come. She'll have to give in like smoke, if I
come only with my credentials, and my honest
trade as well."

What was it that had happened that light, hazy,
summer evening, when the waterfall thundered out
beneath the bridge, when the trees seemed to swell
with new budding leaves, and the sun glittered on
the windows here and there? Was he intoxicated,
or was it the evening that had taken an extra
Midsummer carouse? The last he saw of Silla was
that she hurried homewards with her can, and that
she had looked round at him, as she turned into the
road among the houses.

The world was right enough after all. When he
reckoned it up properly, it was not at all so un-
reasonable, even if the lock did sometimes get out
of order; and then—well, then one had to be both
strong and neat-handed to get it open again.

No, it was right enough. You only see that
when you get inside, and so there must be police
and masters and order in everything, so that it can
lock.

Nikolai stood riveting and meditating down in
the smithy. He had now got his journeyman's
credentials, and everything was rose-colour. The

fact that he and the world were becoming reconciled
showed in shining characters over the whole of his
broad face. His short, strong figure moved with a
newly-acquired, quick confidence at his work.

He worked now for journeyman's wages, and could
save up a nice little sum each week. One fortunate
circumstance in the case was that he never dared
make Silla a present of anything, neither hand-
kerchiefs nor anything else, because of Mrs. Holman.
A penny saved is a penny gained, and she should
have it all in good time.

On Saturday evenings, as soon as he had had a
little wash in the cooling-water, he took his way up
towards the manufacturing part of the town. He
carried his hammer and pincers, and an iron plate
or a lock in his hand ; he must look as if he were
engaged in his lawful work. And then came the
chance whether on his way up or down he caught a
glimpse of Silla.

It was quite a chance, and it sometimes happened
that he just met Mrs. Holman instead. He must
put up with that ; at any rate, he looked right into
the street there, in the cluster of houses where Silla
walked several times a day. But what he found
more difficult to put up with was, that on those
occasions when he was fortunate, she was walking
arm-in-arm with two or three other factory-girls, so
that he scarcely got more than the one glimpse and
short nod from her before they turned in now here,
now there.

What did she want to go loitering about in the evening with those dissipated girls for? Was that the sort of thing for Silla? She was neither old enough nor wise enough to understand what she was getting mixed up in, and what a fine gentleman meant who nodded to her—for the sake of her pretty eyes. Amuse themselves? Yes, go round in the mill, until they come out crushed and ground!

No! She must come out of this.

And so he must work away with his file, and add one week's earnings to another, until he had made the silver hook large enough to draw her to him.

Yes, once she was with him!—he forgot himself in thoughts about house-rent and wedding outlay.

CHAPTER VIII

AN UNEXPECTED ARRIVAL

SOME time after Nikolai had got his credentials, he was pleasantly surprised by a visitor—he could hardly believe his own eyes—none other than his mother, who was watching for him one Saturday afternoon, outside the basement where he dined.

She had heard that he had become a journeyman, and could not rest until she got a lift on one of the plank-loads which was going in to town, and paid him a visit. She was so glad. If he knew how many sighs she had heaved for his sake, and how many bitter tears she had shed—the big, handsome, half peasant-clad woman was red in the face, and wept and dried her eyes incessantly on her folded pocket-handkerchief, while she gave expression to her emotion and joy over the way in which everything had turned out, as if by special guidance.

She had been so unfortunate for a long time; but now that she had got her son again, everything looked different for her. Oh, how big and broad and fine he had grown—a regular smith! He had a frock-coat now for Sundays, hadn't he? And he must have a hat, too. He must let her advise him; she knew all about it from what she had seen in the world.

It was with quite strange, at first almost mixed, feelings that Nikolai thus suddenly saw a mother fall down to him—some day a father might come tumbling down too!

It was so many years since he had thought of her, and the picture he really had of her was buried in the bitter salt slough of tears in the depths of his recollections, which he was far from being in the mood to stir up. There were things within him, which he avoided from an instinctive feeling of safety in the whole of his new, happy existence; but such a thing as finding his mother again must surely belong to the happiness of the new Nikolai, the journeyman smith! Yes, of course, he was fond of her, and it was immensely affecting.

And while he walked beside her, and was glad too, and kind and obliging, and gave up his Saturday afternoon with half a day's pay, he had, without exactly intending it, spent on a present—an exceedingly large, gay, flowered silk handkerchief—as much as it had taken him a fortnight to scrape together; and, besides that, had paid for some fine bread and a ham, which she had to take back with her, and of which she even tried a few goodly slices down in the town by way of afternoon refreshment.

She had an appetite, and she could not be very much accustomed to economising either;—this was about the sum of the happy, filial comments that Nikolai made to himself after the meeting. In addition to this, he felt himself unexpectedly lightened of a good deal of money; and it was in a rather dispirited mood that he went up in the evening in the hope of seeing Silla, and telling her of his new happiness.

The whole of that side of the town up under the hill already lay in shadow, and in the oppressively warm evening, labourers were walking with their coats over their shoulders, while sounds of life and noise rose here and there from the shops in the manufacturing district below.

Nikolai had traversed in vain the district surrounding the Valsets' cottage, keeping constant watch at the same time down the broad high-road, which went past the gate, and the footpath that crept straight across the field down behind it. Silla was not to be seen. A girl went with a bucket from the cow-shed into the pent-house. She looked up towards him and laughed, and the consequence was that Nikolai continued his way towards the factory without once turning round. They must be able to see through the walls in there! And they had already begun to wonder at his coming there so often.

The waterfall was turned off, so that only a white streak ran over the dam and fell drop by drop upon the wheel. A cart was rattling along the road in front of him. Now it stopped to unload; the load was tumbled off with one tilt. It was mould that they were driving to the garden outside the office building at the factory.

Within the fence were a number of women and girls busily at work. They were raking, pulling up and planting, while a man followed with a hose; and out of the open window, with his straw hat on his head, hung young Veyergang, and talked.

There stood Mrs. Holman, with arms akimbo, beside one of the black flower-beds, inspecting some plant that she had patted down with her hand; and —Silla! on her knees, pulling up weeds into her apron from a bed close to the house. It was with her Veyergang was joking from the window, and she shook her head and laughed, and looked up for a moment—she dared not answer because of Mrs. Holman.

It was as if a pair of pincers with many claws had suddenly taken hold of Nikolai's heart, and he all at once remembered so vividly the day when he had had Ludvig Veyergang under his fists.

He went back with a weight like lead upon his breast, and sat down on the edge of a ditch in the field, whence he could, unseen, keep an eye upon all who came down the road.

She had looked so much too pretty when she raised her head with that suppressed merriment in her glance. This was what his thoughts would return to, and he only saw before him what he suffered from.

An hour had passed. Almost stupidly he had watched one after another come down the road; but all at once his face changed colour. Ludvig Veyergang was sauntering past, dashing and easy, with his stick held loosely in his hand. He had red cheeks like a girl, and fine black whiskers beneath the straw hat, and he half closed his grey eyes to look about him, while he hummed softly.

Nikolai gazed despondently after him, as he disappeared down the road.

Again this same old hopelessness before a superior force, this feeling for which he could never find words and vent, unless it some day happened that— he closed his eyes, and there was a compressed, violent expression about his mouth and chin.

There came Silla by Mrs. Holman's side, with bent head, like a willow that is bowed by its growth. Sometimes she stole a glance around, like a school-girl who avoids her teacher's eye.

They separated at the Valsets' cottage; Silla went in after the evening's milk.

She came out again with the can, and took the path over the meadow. She went quickly, smiling to herself, and an almost frightened expression came into her face when Nikolai rose out of the bush by the ditch.

"Do you start when you see me, Silla?"

"How fierce you look!" she answered jestingly.

"You did say you'd be my wife, didn't you, Silla?"

"What makes you say that now, Nikolai? It's such a long time to then."

"I may need to hear it once more. When you aren't more sure than I am, you like to feel twice whether the strap you are holding on to is firmly fastened, or if it will give way. You have got so much into your head since you came up here to the factory."

"Take care! Just you take care, Nikolai. You have become so dreadfully afraid for me lately," she said, laughing saucily; "but I've become a little grown-up too. It's only you who don't see it, and stand there like a post! But you can't think how awfully busy I am now. As soon as ever I've swallowed my supper, I go up to the factory again. I and Kristofa and Kalla and Josefa have got the whole of the weeding and tidying up in the office garden, down all the peas and carrots, and cabbage-beds as well; and when it grows over in the autumn, we shall have that too."

Nikolai only stood reckoning. Twenty-seven dollars, subtracting what he had spent on his mother to-day—the ham, too, for he would not get that back—that was what he owned, and he needed at least twice as much again before he could get the most necessary things for his room. Only to get her out of this, even if he had to work day and night.

Aloud he only said cautiously: "If we are only wise, and careful, and look well ahead, perhaps we

may be sitting in our own room by next spring,
Silla. But so many things may happen in between,"
he added huskily, with a deep-drawn sigh.

"I really believe there'll be neither life nor
courage in you until you're married, Nikolai," she
said, laughing; "you're so horrid to meet now, that
it's enough to make one quite sad and uncomfortable
the whole evening. A nice sweetheart you are!"
She swung roguishly round on her heel, with the
can extended, and ran down the road, nodding a
farewell.

He had not got so far as to tell her what he had
originally gone up there for—the news about his
mother, and, to tell the truth, he had completely
forgotten it; but it would be time enough next time
he met her. And it must not be too long to that,
things looking as they did now.

      *   *   *   *   *

A few weeks afterwards some one inquired for
him.

A peasant carter, in a state of great uncertainty
about his load, had stopped outside the eating-house.
Part of the load was made up of his mother's big
chest, which the man had undertaken to drive to
town, and leave for the meantime at Nikolai's.
Barbara herself was to follow in a day or two.

She must have some project in her head!
Perhaps she was thinking of going out to service
again.

And one evening when he came home he found a red wooden box and a pair of laced boots upon the chest. His mother must have been there!

Half an hour later she appeared. She had only been out to buy a little new rye-bread, cheese, and butter to take up to her lodgings this evening.

In the meantime she cut some for herself and offered some to him.

Her ample figure, in addition to her effects, almost filled Nikolai's narrow little bedroom. She had become rather short of breath, and acquired a double-chin with so much sitting indoors; the lower part of her face, which, in the brilliancy of youth, had been covered with pure, healthy mountain roses, now, as it moved in the process of eating, gave only the impression of powerful crushing with still solid teeth, in which, however, toothache, from many scalding cups of coffee, had made here and there serious inroads. While she sat on the chest and he on the bed, she gave expression to the following:

The farmer with whom she had bargained to live —for eighteen dollars a year and help at the busy seasons, while she found herself in coffee—was so pinching and mean about the board, that she had been obliged to buy one thing and another herself; well, he had seen the ham himself, and knew what she had been accustomed to at the Veyergangs'. She could truly say that she had swallowed her food with tears many a time, when she thought of all that she had done for Ludvig and Lizzie, that she had carried them in her arms and been more to them than their own mother. And then to think that the reward of all this should be hard work in the hay and corn harvest! No, she was praised by too many mouths for that!

She had waited patiently, too, thinking they would remember old Barbara. Oh no! one would have to remind them one's self, if that were to be!

But now that she had Nikolai there, she had thought and meditated and reflected about setting up a little shop in the town. And she had been out to the Consul's to-day.

He was cross when she went into the office, and snappish; but she knew him, and began talking cleverly:

"How is mistress and Mr. Ludvig and Miss Lizzie, might I be so bold as to ask? Bless me, they must have grown so tall and so grand now, that they couldn't be expected to know a poor servant again!"

"'Thin—thin as laths,' he laughed. 'You might easily hold them one in each arm now! But you must have eaten up the whole barn up there; I didn't remember that you were so big, Barbara. I should think he's had to give up house and lands, that farmer?' he said, to tease me.

"'Thank you, I wasn't accustomed to cattle fodder at the Consul's house,' said I; 'and it's me, rather, that's in such circumstances that I must leave. That man takes pretty good care that he is not cheated.'

"And then I talked abcut Ludvig and Lizzie until I began to cry.

"'And that harum-scarum boy of yours?' he asked.

"'Thank you,' said I, 'my son Nikolai is now a finished journeyman smith in this city.'

"And then I told him my thoughts of coming to town to go into trade. 'I have always noticed that it has been better to be behind the counter than in front of it,' I said.

"Then he laughed. 'You want to make yourself a new storehouse in town, I see, Barbara.'

"'Yes, sir, when it can be done honestly, and with a little help; every one aims at their own mainten-ance.'

"And then he promised me right down a free room and kitchen in one of the houses up in the manu-facturing part of the town for a whole year!"

As mother and son sat opposite to one another, they were not without a certain similarity; but where the leading of fate had turned the features of his broad, intelligent face into muscle and energy, it had in Barbara relaxed all the springs into dull, ponderous fat.

It was not, however, without a certain amount of enthusiasm that she now unfolded her plans for the little business, and how she should procure credit, a little at each place; she still had acquaintances at the shops in the neighbourhood, from the time she was at the Veyergangs'. Afterwards it was only to sell out, pay for the old, get new again; it all went round like a winch!

But she must have a little more ready money, for hers would not go far enough. Now, if Nikolai could help her with a little; it would all lie in the goods, so that, for that matter, it was the same whether he put his pence there or in his pocket—the same to a T!

Could he tell her where she could buy a counter cheap! Or rather, get it on credit; if there was anything she was hard up for now, it was ready money. Perhaps she might as well try to take out a little more at the carpenter's at once, only a fair-sized folding-table, two beds, and a few chairs. She had thought that when once she had got it started and into order, Nikaloi might live with her. If she prepared all his meals for him besides, the one thing might be set off against the other, and part of his wages go towards it—he must himself reckon up and say how much he thought.

Barbara continued more eagerly to build up in her own mind, and emphasising now and then with a smack of her hand, how everything was to be.

But as she waxed warmer and more elated over her visions of the future, Nikolai sat doubtful, and softly beating a measure with his foot. All this about the shop might be right enough. His mother must surely understand it, she who had been at the

Veyergangs', and had now, moreover, talked to the Consul himself. But the more she initiated him into her plans, and in them appropriated him entirely to herself, and talked away as if there could be no obstacle in any corner of the heavens, the wider did the gulf between their wills and interests open before him. She came with a mother's long-dispensed-with right, and just now he knew in his heart that he belonged still more to another, and must go his own way.

She could not know that she was coming upon nails the whole time in the wall, so he would have to speak out.

"Well, you see, mother"—he looked down at the floor—"you're welcome to my money, if only it's certain I get it back again by the new year, so there's nothing to hinder that. But, you know, why I must have it again is—is because I and Mrs. Holman's Silla have agreed to marry and settle down. And I'm quite determined about it, for I've worked and toiled for that, ever since Holman died; and it would be ill for me if I had to be without her."

His sharp, grey eyes shot a glance up at her, and the mother instinctively felt that here was a will that had escaped from her hands.

This was something that had never entered into her plans.

In order to remove her dissatisfaction, he let her have his thirty dollars before she went.

There is a branch of trade in the narrow streets
and outskirts, whose position is one storey higher
than the stall-woman. It sells its wares from a
house, comprises, according to legislation, a great
many more effects, and allows the individual concerned to lead a more comfortable existence, with a
step farther from hand to mouth ; that is to say, it
gains, instead of a day's credit or a weekly settlement, a week's credit or a monthly settlement.

It was in this small trade that Barbara wanted to
start, and if it can be said of America that whole
towns and undertakings arise in a moment of time,
something of the same kind might well be said of
Barbara's shop.

Barely a week later she was in her house, and
had in the window an exhibition of balls of cotton,
bread, twists, sweets, stay-laces, needle-cases, snuff,
clay pipes, steel pens, matches, etc., etc., while she
herself sat behind the counter—which was a packing-
case disguised under some print—and ground coffee,
which she roasted in the kitchen beyond. In a
drawer that would lock, which Nikolai had over-
looked, stood the cigar-box that did duty as a cash-
box, with a few coppers in it.

The acquaintance between Mrs. Holman and
Barbara, too, was already renewed, with the secret
about Silla preserved on Barbara's side.

Mrs. Holman—she lived only in the street below
—had come up, while Barbara was standing on her
steps in the evening, to look at her new surroundings

by the light of the just completed shop-window. And then she must not pass an old acquaintance's door. She must come in and have a cup of coffee —it was standing clearing on the hob, if she would condescend.

Mrs. Holman might very well have had her own opinion about a good deal that she saw in there, but she preferred, while she drank her coffee, to give Barbara some idea of the series of dispensations which she had passed through since Holman died.

"Oh no, don't turn your cup up yet! *One* more, Mrs. Holman."

Mrs. Holman drank a third cup too, without becoming at all less melancholy. Her quiet, cold grey eyes had looked and explored while she talked, and sucked in observations of Barbara's open-handed, profuse management, like pipe-clayed fat. But when she left, she had, with many cautious reservations, and in the hope that Barbara's wares would stand the test in the long run, expressed her inclination to remove her custom to Barbara.

Mrs. Holman's Silla was just standing at the counter—she wanted a pint of groats to take home with her—when Barbara, who was measuring them out, suddenly saw Ludvig Veyergang at the door.

He had seen Barbara before, and as he passed the door twice a day now, he nodded to her whenever she showed herself on the steps. But so friendly as he was to-day! Barbara was quite softened, and very nearly called him Ludvig, he was so lively and playful about her shop. He stood looking with half-closed eyes, and laughing at Silla, who grew redder and more bashful, and only tried in her confusion to get the bag of groats out of Barbara's hand. He had taken his straw hat off his curly hair for the heat, and looked so nice and handsome.

Silla hardly dared look up at him, and only heard something about freckles not being anything to mind when one had such dark eyes, when, with head in advance, she rushed out of the door.

Barbara's opinion afterwards about Silla's behaviour—her having all at once turned crimson, and rushed away at a few innocent words from such a well-meaning and handsome man as Ludvig Veyergang—her son heard the same evening. A young girl ought to stand modestly, and not go on like that : if she did, it was a sure way of getting all that could be called man-folk at her heels.

Was she anything for Nikolai—that awkward, dark, long girl, who ran about in that bodice that was too short for her, looking like a half-peeled, bent prawn in the back, and went balancing along the edge of the gutter, as if she were going to be a tight-rope dancer—without any education ? Upon her word, if it had been any other than Ludvig Veyergang, she would have had him peeping after her at every corner.

"But, do you know, Nikolai, it suddenly came into my head while he stood there, that here was the person who both could and would help me with those fifteen dollars I still want so badly. But he was gone before I could collect myself."

"Him? N—no, mother! I'll get them for you, if you'll only wait a little; and I think you can use my money as well as his."

"Well, if I hadn't got you, Nikolai!" sighed Barbara, moved; "and now you shall have some coffee that's good, and new cinnamon-sticks with it, that I didn't get sold to-day."

"No, thanks all the same, mother," he answered, gloomily: he was already at the door.

Later in the evening he succeeded in meeting Silla. She was so merry and laughing this evening.

"I ran away; didn't look at him at all. Would you have liked me to stay, perhaps?" she said, playfully.

He was disarmed for the moment, she laughed so confidingly.

But as he went down, he still saw Veyergang's insolent, half-closed eyes, and the curl coming out beneath his hat, and—he could not help it—he felt as if it were twined round his finger!

That she chattered so gaily did not please him, nor yet that whenever he made time to go up in the evening she came down breathless from the garden, and was always full of whether young Veyergang had been there or not, what he had said, and what she had thought, and whether Kristofa had afterwards agreed or disagreed with her. It was as if she could not talk of anything else!

Yet it was not so bad, he supposed, so long as it was she herself who chattered and talked about it to him.

But the perspiration would stream from him in the smithy, when he stood and thought about it all up there. He felt as though he were under a screw.

Why should not the poor man's possession be left in peace? Here he was toiling away, and would give every drop of blood in his body to be able to marry; and that other one, who had his pockets full, and could have any fine lady for the asking— they were worse than wild beasts and murderers! And amidst all this the time was passing.

He had blessed both the autumn mud and darkness, which put an end to all the running about in the evening; and now winter days and snow had come. When he reckoned up—and he was always reckoning—he found that by the New Year he would be worth seventy-five specie-dollars—what he had almost starved himself to save—and of these his mother had had forty-five, and since then thirteen more. He had made a half bargain about a room with a kitchen at a fair price per month, and what he wanted for the house, too. The last time he had lent his mother money, she had said that he need not be afraid, she was selling the goods and sweeping in the profits.

Everything was in order, so the battle with Mrs. Holman had better be fought at once. And when he laid before her his journeyman's credentials, his seventy-five dollars, and his regular earnings, with the advance he was to have from the New Year at Hægberg's, she would have to be so kind as to give in.

It was on one of the days between Christmas and the New Year that he went up to his mother to let her know that he must have his money out in February. Then he would go to Mrs. Holman.

It struck him that his mother was rather confused and forgetful while she made the coffee.

She thought she was half crazy to-day, she said; but he should have his coffee. and Christmas should not pass without his having something good; it had not been the custom where she was brought up.

Oh, dear! So Nikolai wanted his money back already. She had grown so forgetful, that she had not remembered that it was so soon. And just before Christmas she had had to settle a bill for coffee and sugar which, upon her word, she had not thought or known would come in until after the fair or at Midsummer! But he need not be afraid; she knew well enough where she could get the money, if she liked to tie on her bonnet and go out after it.

"So drink, Nikolai; it's as strong as a rock. It isn't Christmas more than once a year, as they say in the country. I believe you're afraid. For your money? Oh, no; never you fear! If your mother, Barbara, has promised anything, she'll keep it; so you may be easy. So nice as Ludvig was to me the last time he was in here—it was only the afternoon of Little Christmas Eve.* Barbara needn't be at a loss for a few pence when I say my son wants them. Oh, dear no! Now, Nikolai, don't look like that. Don't you hear you shall have it? My goodness, how you do look at me!"

He said nothing, only sat still a long time, and Barbara thought it was getting oppressively quiet. She tried first one thing and then another.

"I'll try it directly after New Year. I would never have borrowed your money if I'd known it would be like this."

"No, mother. You must pay me the money when you can; I won't press you for it. But if you try to beg it from Ludvig Veyergang, we are parted for this world, and as far as I get into the next, too! So now you know, mother. And many thanks for the wedding this time, both from me and Silla!" and he pulled open the door.

* The day before Christmas Eve proper.

CHAPTER IX

AN IMPORTANT STEP TAKEN

IF Silla had not come like a wedge between the bark and the wood, how comfortably and free from care Barbara could have lived now. She had no one but Silla to thank that she was now deprived of all the help she might and—it was her firm conviction—ought to have had in her son Nikolai, with the regular earnings he might have put, every single week, into the till; which, for some reason or other, never would exhibit the amount it ought to have done.

It was not improbable that Barbara, after the fashion of country people, forgot to take into account the articles that went towards the nourishment of her own weighty person. On the other hand her ever ready hospitality with the coffee-pot was not without its savour of trade-policy—what she gave away was only to be looked upon as seed which would bring forth a hundredfold in the shape of customers.

Barbara's room was thus becoming the meeting-

place for all the gossiping forces of the neighbourhood.

   *   *   *   *

The posts in the fences had snow hats on, and
snow-drifts lay by the roadside and on the fields.

One afternoon, when the sledges were creaking
outside in the cold, and the door too, whenever
anybody came in, Mother Taraldsen, who cupped
people and applied leeches, and tall Mother Bækken
were sitting and enjoying a cup of steaming hot
coffee with loaf-sugar.

Mother Taraldsen was holding forth on the subject
of bad liquids and ruined times, and how every trade
was going down-hill, while Mother Bækken, getting
more and more full of objections, put her head on
one side, and stirred up her cup.

"I can remember a little of the old times too,
and I don't know if they were any better, though
every one is welcome to have his opinion, of course,"
here the long, yellow face with the eyes blinking
with their own meaning, was laid almost across the
cup; "but the day has grown longer for workmen
now. Just think how they sat in the dark in the
farms and cottages with pine-torches in the fire-
place to cut and spin by; and there lay the lads the
whole long winter through, and idled and yawned
in their beds from three or four in the afternoon
until they had to go out with a lantern and see to
the horses for the night. But paraffine has got
them out of their beds. It's as if we had the sun

the whole winter now, and people can see to earn a few pence."

"Yes, but everything hasn't got right in that way either, when they sit and play cards and gamble and drink at the public-houses."

"That's not oil, that's gas! But that's good for something, too, both in the street lamps and up in the factory."

"And for drunkenness and dancing and wickedness."

Mother Bækken made a bend down to her cup with the side of her cheek and her chin, and up again in order to contradict in her most ingenious manner. But just then Anne Graves came in to the counter—it was she who kept the churchyard in order—and then one must be careful what one says.

Thank you kindly! She had no objection to a warm cup of coffee in this cold. She had had a busy day to-day with the big funeral; they must have heard all the ringing at dinner-time. He was an excellent man. She enlarged, by the plundering of diverse fragments of the funeral sermon, upon his worth and importance as a man and a citizen of the town. There had been speeches and such countless black hats and flowers, that the coffin was quite hidden. Yes, that was the third they had taken in since the New Year, she uttered with a sigh.

"You never know what sort of people you have among you, until they are dead," remarked Mother

Bækken. " If he had been the poor man's friend,
they could have sung and trumpeted a little about it
while he lived. Perhaps that's turned the wrong
way, but——" she slowly, and with increasing
expression, bent her face over her cup.

Mother Bækken must always have her own in-
terpretations, so Mother Taraldsen discreetly warded
off a disturbance of the peace by striking into the
very middle of the manufacturing part of the town.
She had come up the streets yesterday evening with
a covered cup containing leeches, and you might
really think that if, all that long way up from the
chemist's, you had escaped rogues and robbers, you
ought to go free up here. But there came those
great, grown-up girls, flying one after another along
a slide down the street, screaming and shouting, so
that it was enough to knock people down. So she
had dropped the cup with all five leeches in it, and if
it had not been moonlight so that she could see to
pick them up again on the snow, she would have
lost every single one. It was that Josefa and Gunda
and Kalla down the street, and that long Silla—
she came along like a ghost. Ah, Mrs. Holman,
who is so particular, should see what sort of a
daughter she has, when it gets dark.

Barbara nodded to herself, and thought that
Nikolai should just hear what people said.

"I must really go out and look at them one
evening, yes indeed. Well, that about the leeches
I disapprove of entirely and altogether, I must

confess. But young blood must have movement in some way, and may· I ask,"—here Mother Bœkken laid one fore-finger upon the other—"have they any way of amusing themselves, if they must *not* dance, and *not* slide, and *not* toboggan ?"

But now Mother Taraldsen grew angry.

"If it's proper for respectable young girls to tear about and make a row, it must be the new fashion that Mother Bœkken's preaching about. If you kept a careful watch at the corners, you might perhaps see that there were those who were out to meet the flock of geese."

"Then it would be better if you came down on *them* instead of the poor girls," replied Mother Bœkken obstinately; "a man like that clerk down at the contractor's, and him at the Stores, and then that fine clerk, that Veyergang up at the factory and his friends."

Barbara was standing at the counter with a customer.

Nobody must say anything against her Ludvig. She knew him; she had been with him day and night for fourteen years. If she only had a half-penny for every time he had cried and screamed for Barbara !

She would have enlarged upon the subject, if it had not been for the man at her back who was calling out for his soft soap.

So cup-and-leech-Mother Taraldsen went on, saying that the girls stood poking their heads out of every single gate the whole way up the street; she saw it so well when she came home from applying leeches of an evening.

She and Anne Graves then began to review the young people more closely. There were some they would not even mention, and some they named with all sorts of interesting doubts and opinions, and lastly some they only stopped to wonder that they had nothing whatever to say either about or against.

As to Barbara, she noticed carefully what was said about Silla, and made up her mind that Nikolai should be warned; he should at any rate know what he was doing when he went and took that girl.

And neither was it with a diminishing-glass she let him see it, as time after time she referred to all the dangers the young factory-girls up there were exposed to. She had sufficient instinct not to mention Silla, so that he should not think she was speaking against her. But every time she touched upon it, she saw well, that it went into Nikolai, and had fully the effect she wished.

Barbara had made some of these remarks this evening too, and Nikolai was sitting gloomily listening to the noise outside.

One party after another was flying past down the high-road on sledges, like shadows in the moonlight, with shouts and cries—half-grown lads and lassies, and now and then a party of fine people from the town below. One tall lad, with the rope over his shoulder and his heels digging into the hill-side, was dragging a wood-sledge up, with a heavy load of girls upon it.

Nikolai could not help keeping watch through the kitchen window, and left his mother, who sat inside by the paraffine lamp, without any answer.

They were Kristofa and Kalla, those two who were standing there in the street talking, while they slid backwards and forwards the whole time on a little bit of ice. They were waiting for somebody—Silla perhaps; they were standing close by her street. It was a question which of them would dare to venture in and be so bold as to ask Mrs. Holman with many "dear, kind, goods" if she would allow Silla to go over to her for a little while this evening—always untruthfulness and disorder!

There was another sledge party with fine hats and glowing cigars standing laughing just outside.

Barbara stopped her knitting-pins to listen.

"We have this noise every evening till quite late," she remarked, "as long as the moon shines on the road."

He turned hot all over. If Silla were to get into this, then he might as well lay both himself and his hammer down.

Yes, there she was looking about at the corner for her two friends.

"Good evening, old lady," said he, suddenly coming out of the door.

"Is that you, Nikolai?" exclaimed Silla, in surprise. "Have you seen anything of Kristofa and

Kalla? I did so want to speak to them! Haven't
you? Do you know how I got out? I was only
going to get the cat in for the night. I chased it
out myself, and hid it so nicely under the wooden
tub out in the shed. If only it doesn't mew."

She looked round again eagerly, while the elon-
gated shadow across the snow imitated her slender
figure and swaying movements.

"Oh, and they promised to wait for me!"

"Well, I suppose they've only gone."

"Only? They thought I was going out with them
this evening, and if they haven't been here already,
they may perhaps stand and wait, for I must go in,
you see, or else I shall have mother coming out into
the street after me. Listen, Nik! If you were
nice"—she took hold of his jacket, and pushed him
backwards and forwards—"you would find them and
tell them—can you tell them properly?—that I must
be good and stay at home this evening, but hurrah
for a holiday to-morrow and the day after! Say
that mother will be washing at the Antonisens' the
whole of the end of the week, and they'll quite
understand it. But be sure you find them, Nikolai,
so that they won't blame me."

Nikolai was not insensible to her amiability, nor
yet to her liveliness and prettiness; but it had just
the opposite effect. While she stood pulling his
jacket, he heard the voices on the high-road all the
time.

"That's it, that's it! You want to get quite free

now, Silla. Well, just let them drag you out among them! But that a respectable girl will let herself be drawn into such goings on!" he added, out of humour.

"A respectable girl? Respectable girl! May I ask what sort of fun she is to have then? I really wonder, Nikolai, that you didn't find a respectable girl for yourself who would walk with her back like a poker, and her arms under her shawl, and who only lets herself slide by accident as it were, when she comes to a slide—daren't even look out of the corner of her eye at a hand-sledge, because she's so well-behaved! It was a respectable one like that you ought to have had. And then, when you were standing hammering all day in the smithy, and she was deep in her work standing on all fours with her head behind the wash-tub at home, I suppose that would be as you would like to have it. But I can tell you, Nikolai, that if there isn't to be any fun in this world, then good-bye and be rid of it. I've had to sit shut up long enough at home."

He shook his head. "If only there weren't all those wolves howling away there on the road. But you see, they want to amuse themselves too ; and— and the insignificant ones have to take care of what they have, it seems to me—and if you're of the same mind, Silla, we'll go in to your mother at once—this very moment." He took her by the hand to carry out his intention.

"You must be mad, Nikolai," she exclaimed in

terror; the resolution was as terrible as it was unexpected. "No, no, let it be," she begged in an eager
whisper. "Think of mother! Have you quite
forgotten what mother is like? It will be time
enough when we've got something to marry on."

"Time enough? No, it's not time enough for
me, Silla. I must try and get it said now."

"And what will happen to me at home afterwards? And you're not dressed for it either, this
evening."

"Oh, don't be afraid, Mr. Nikolai. I may as well
see with my own eyes how highly my daughter con-
descends to respect her mother who is left a poor
defenceless widow."

It was Mrs. Holman's own voice; she was
standing in the gateway, looking preternaturally
large.

"I thought I had gone through the worst that
could be, when Holman died, and that I should be
spared the pain of catching my own flesh and blood
out, without leave, in conversation in the street, in the
middle of the snow. Neither should I have thought
that that person would ever presume to come so near
my house. Just you come in with me, Silla. Come
in, do you hear—at once!"

If any one could have gathered up the component
parts of Mrs. Holman's last screaming treble, he
would have found a wealth of emotions: injured
motherly dignity, wrath, contempt, hatred, and
something heavy, which was meant to have a

crushing effect, and really did almost make Silla fall on her knees ; she stood there without moving.

Nikolai had become a little hardened, however, since the old days ; he knew now that there were others of whom he was more afraid than he was of Mrs. Holman. He was not affected by her.

"I must ask to be allowed to come in, however, ma'am, for I didn't come here this evening to stand out in the snow. It is to you yourself I want to speak."

"Perhaps it's no longer than can be said here where we stand," answered Mrs. Holman, rudely. "Come here, Silla ! "

"Oh no, it's not very long ; but then I must explain one or two things that belong to it."

As Mrs. Holman still continued to bar the gateway and only beckoned again to her daughter, Silla, in her despair and terror, suddenly made her choice. There was nothing for it but to shut her eyes and stand by Nikolai, and she took his arm boldly.

"Yes, ma'am, that's it, as you see. We hold together as we have done ever since we were little. And I came this evening to ask for her, and to ask if we could have the benefit of your leave and consent. For with my credentials and good wages, and when I never drink and——"

Silla now acted with the courage of despair ; she pushed Nikolai so that they all three—Mrs.

Holman yielding half involuntarily—came through the gate and from thence into the room where the battle was then fought.

While Silla sat with her hands before her face on a chair in the dark and Nikolai, with quiet persistency continued to plead his case, and make as manifest as possible how he now had a prospect of becoming foreman and could provide for Silla, Mrs. Holman assumed a mightily offended, repellant attitude. She employed her whole power; she bridled, and she was wrathful, and she exhibited the most extreme astonishment. It almost looked as if he thought he could really take her daughter from her, whether she said yes or no. What was there left for an elderly woman to live on, when her husband was dead, and her daughter who could keep her, refused, because she thought of marrying a smith who could not so much as show that he had a wedded father?

She was on the point of rising in defence to the death of her maternal rights, when a light suddenly dawned upon her. Her eyes began to gaze into a perspective of the future. If Nikolai ever came to justify the great words and promises he was now making, she might, in case of the worst, when the time came, claim an asylum with them.

This thought, however, did not prevent her from selling every concession, with deep sighs, as dearly as possible.

She must say she had thought of something quite different for Silla. And, however it might be, she would not hear of any gadding about or sweet-hearting until Nikolai could show as much ready money as Holman had done.

He had had a hundred dollars and his good wages, and when Nikolai could lay as much money on the table in front of her eyes, it would be time to talk about it.

A hundred dollars—that was something decided at last. He held her in a vice with that.

That was the feeling which filled him when, a little while after, he sprang right across the snow-drift to shorten the way, and knocked at Barbara's door. He must have some one to tell it to—that Mrs. Holman had acquiesced in Silla's having in this way promised herself to him.

It was exactly the same view of her well-con-sidered advantage that occurred to Barbara while she lay that night collecting herself after the news. She raised her large person up in bed under the influence of the brilliant idea :

Why, then, she could live with Nikolai !

This grocery business was completely eating her up—it did not enter her head that she was eating *it* up.

She suddenly felt quite clear as to her whole position ; how it would be best both for her and Nikolai that she should give up the shop in time, and how instead she could be of unspeakable use in helping the totally inexperienced Silla to manage the house, and perhaps earn a few pence at other houses. And she had never heard but that a son was bound to provide for his mother.

The following Sunday Mrs. Holman drank coffee at Barbara's; but as Mrs. Holman was silent about what had taken place, Barbara was silent too. Only once she led the conversation up to her son Nikolai, and thought that possibly in the autumn, when the room next door was empty, he might move into it. It would not be too much, when it was remembered how they had always been separated.

Why Mrs. Holman at that moment became thoughtful, pursed up her mouth and said: "Thank you," she would not have any more coffee! and somewhat unexpectedly shortened her visit, shall be left untold. It can only be stated, that from that moment, a silent contest began between them under water—under the most friendly form, it must be added, for Mrs. Holman's sake if for nothing else.

The coffee visits continued, if possible, with greater frequency, and Barbara as well as Mrs. Holman discussed and talked over every possible subject, except the one that lay nearest to their hearts—their own personal plans in connection with Nikolai and Silla. On that point they watched each other in diplomatic silence, like two chess-players of whom the one dare not move until he has seen through the other one's intention; Mrs. Holman, in the middle of some strictly reserved opinion, taking in everything with her precise, little face and cold grey eyes, and seeing it all clear and small as if through the bottom of a tumbler; and Barbara, round, hospitable, large and fat, with great, overflowing features, and generally talking about her time at the Consul's.

But during all this, there was one thing upon which each of them became always more and more decided—if she could not live with them herself, she would at any rate put a stop to the other coming and filling up the house.

The two future mothers-in-law were each occupied to the best of their ability in making it impossible for the other; but of this quietly calculated conflict which was going on in the ground far below them, Nikolai and Silla had no suspicion.

CHAPTER X

A RISE IN LIFE

SINCE Mrs. Holman had seen what Silla could busy herself with—she was quite struck with amazement at her own blindness—she had become far more strictly attentive, and also much more on the lookout and watch against Nikolai.

The fruits of idleness had unfortunately revealed themselves, and there was no other remedy for them than to watch conscientiously and see that Silla worked. She must really set about something that there was some use and help in, all through the long light spring evenings, and not just run for the milk, or out when any one came and asked if she might.

Nikolai soon found that the situation was far from being improved after he was acknowledged in the quality of wooer. But notwithstanding that he saw no more of her than a short glimpse now and then, a great step in advance had actually been made. He had now only to work hard, and that he did manfully; the hammer worked, in his hands, as if by steam.

In some ways, too, he was reassured, for if Mrs. Holman watched against him so carefully, this same watchfulness was a security against others, too. It was well to know that she was no longer to be found up there among those giddy girls in the evening. A cold shiver ran down his back when he one day met young Veyergang coming out of his mother's. He only looked indifferently at Nikolai with half-closed eyes, when they met in the doorway, as if he did not quite remember him, and then asked Barbara over his shoulder, with a nod at Nikolai: "Is that the fellow?" and went out:

"What's he been doing here, mother?"

"Nothing."

"Have you been borrowing money of him?" he continued sharply.

"Of course not. Not a penny, though I do need it so badly."

"What was he talking about?"

"He wanted to light his cigar, as he so often does when he goes down this way. Surely that can't do you any harm! And it wouldn't be much good forbidding him to do it either, I should think—either for me or for you!" She added the last words red with anger.

"No, I certainly can't forbid him, mother. But remember, if you borrow of him, everything is at an end between us!"

"Oh, Nikolai, you are so quick-tempered. No,

of course not; I shouldn't think of borrowing!"
As she spoke she turned round and pushed something she had in her hand into her bosom. "No,
of course not!"

"I could hear he had been talking about
me."

"No, indeed, how could you think so?"

"Yes he was, mother," he persisted, gloomily.

"About you? Oh, well, I was telling him a little
about how hard you were working now to get
together those few shillings for Mrs. Holman."
Barbara talked rather confusedly.

"And perhaps about Silla, too?" he asked search-
ingly.

"Oh, no! he knew all about that before. I'm
not the only one who knows about it in this gossiping place, and, upon my honour, Nikolai, it didn't
come from me—not to-day," she added.

"I wouldn't have minded if you had said it then ;
it would be a good thing for that fellow to know that
she is an engaged girl."

"Isn't that just what I said? Only he didn't
believe it."

"No, I dare say not!" Nikolai stood at the
window reflecting. This visit of Veyergang's!

He had enough noise and worry just now down
at the smithy. It was just a question whether he
should not be made a foreman. Old Mrs. Ellingsen
had sent for him several times on this account, and
it looked as if it were almost settled.

Things had been in this condition for some time; there was no great need of hurry in coming to a determination, as the situation was not to be filled until the autumn.

Lately, however, it had seemed to Nikolai that Mrs. Ellingsen was behaving rather strangely. He noticed, too, that they were talking and making a great deal of fuss in the smithy; but it did not strike him that it might be Mrs. Ellingsen's intention to draw back, until one day when one of the men remarked scornfully that he did not suppose there was any one in the smithy who would think of supplanting Olaves. If any one did, he would have to look out for himself, for they would all stick to Olaves.

Nikolai knew well that they frowned at him because he was always hard at work, saved up his pence, and firmly refused to join the others in a glass of beer or a dram.

He was without a companion. And now, when this foreman's question hung in the balance, he noticed that the whole of his past life was stirred and dug up again till it was as thick as the grounds in a coffee-cup—from the old police and fighting story right back to his childhood's days among the timber-stacks.

These old stories were Nikolai's smarting wounds. He was always thinking they were forgotten, and they were always coming up again, and now it was insupportable suffering. He endeavoured not to betray it by a look; but he was by no means in a good temper as he stood there.

The sooner he got to know from Mrs. Ellingsen how it was to end the better; and Nikolai was soon standing with his cap in his hand in her room, to ask what he might depend upon.

It took a long time, with many "h'ms" and "ha's" before she managed to get her spectacles off and the wires put properly into her hair again. Then at last it came out with some hesitation. She meant no offence; she knew he was a good smith enough; but there were so many who knew Olaves to be such an honest, good fellow, and she was an old woman who needed some one whom she could thoroughly trust—no offence meant to Nikolai—but she must consider the matter.

That was the answer he received, and with it his prospects, that he had counted upon and shown to Mrs. Holman when he asked for Silla's hand, were destroyed.

The next day when he came into the smithy they all smiled and tittered. They knew he had been to Mrs. Ellingsen and had got his answer. But if they thought they could tease or frighten him into giving it up, they were very much mistaken.

Olaves behaved as if nothing was the matter, and even civilly offered a helping-hand in breaking the bar-iron.

Nikolai only turned his back on him.

"I never meddle with any other man's work, and

I don't advise any one to worm himself into my affairs," he said, " unless he wants a dressing that will make his back as hot as that red iron there ! " he added, with a glance at Olaves.

There was a general silence.

But at dinner-time there was a great deal of talking and fuss about this affair. Every one had heard how Nikolai had threatened Olaves, and Olaves, as a precaution, found witnesses for his words.

" He looked as if he could use the sledge-hammer to something besides forging bolts, that fellow, if he could do it without witnesses ! "

They might talk as much as they liked for all that Nikolai cared; he did his work, and never heard that Hægberg had anything to complain of. He was prepared for a disappointment now.

There was one thing, though, that he would do before he gave in—go straight to Hægberg and speak out, and then the master could give his testimony as to which he wanted, if Mrs. Ellingsen asked him.

The final answer from Mrs. Ellingsen was delayed week after week : at last it was two months.

What could the old woman mean ? The whole smithy wondered—she must have a foreman by the autumn.

At last, one morning it appeared in the shape of a message.

It was drawing on towards evening one broiling hot summer day. In both floors of the grey

wooden house in which Mrs. Holman lived, the
small-paned windows stood open, drinking in the
slight coolness there was in the air, while the
dwellers within went about their occupations more
or less lightly clothed. A faint breath only now and
again stirred the half transparent curtains, or the
white clothes hanging on lines across the yard.

At the window on the ground floor just above the
entrance to the cellar, stood a slender, dark-eyed
young girl with turned-up sleeves, busy at the water
tap under which she had a wash-tub full of clothes.
Her head could be seen now above, now below the
short blind, cooled and refreshed by the cold rush
of water.

Suddenly she stopped in surprise.

Nikolai entered with his flat cap pushed triumph-
antly on one side.

"The world's right enough, I can tell you, Silla.
The only thing is to see that everything is properly
in order from the very beginning. He who hasn't
got a father, must be his own father, you know!"

"But Nikolai! Did you know mother was out?"

"Pooh! What is there that I don't know! My
mother told me just now that it was one of the
washing days at Antonisens. But you see, Silla,
it's beginning to get late, and—if you'd like to
know—I've been invited to-day to be foreman at
Mrs. Ellingsen's. That'll be only ten dollars a
month more!"

"Foreman? Is it true, Nikolai?" She retreated

from the wash-tub, looking doubtfully at him.
"Come here with your smutty face!" she said,
hastily pulling the clothes out of the tub. "You
are so awfully black! Foreman, did you say? No,
is it really true? Oh, you must put up with a little
splashing; I can't see the foreman for coal-soot!
Then Mrs. Ellingsen didn't ask Olaves first?"

"No, she didn't."

"And no one put out their tongue or made Mrs
Ellingsen afraid of you, as they did before?"

"Oh, Hægberg must have let her know that he
hadn't taken any harm from me."

"If only they don't begin again and do what they
can. For your getting in front of them stings and
chafes and torments every one of them, ever since
that time when you had to do those wheel pivots
over again for Olaves. And then they dig up all
the old stories they can find."

"Oh no! The world's right enough, I tell you,
and Mrs. Ellingsen must take the smith who works
her smithy best. Besides it's as fixed as a vice, and
the contract signed this morning. And it's pretty
badly needed, for the money that mother borrowed
last, it—it—whu!"—he whistled—"has gone the
same way as the rest. It disappears like smoke with
her. It seems to me she trades backwards instead
of forwards, and that the profits go the wrong way."

"Now you're so nice and clean, that you shine
That way with your hair or else the cock's-comb will
stand up too much."

"I rushed straight out of the smithy, you see, to come up here and cram it into you. I went in to mother first, and then I promised her to go down and buy some mackerel for supper. Two smacks have come in to-day, they say."

Silla's face showed that this was a great piece of news. They were both natives of the town, and the arrival of the mackerel brought with it a number of pleasant recollections and pictures from the time when they lived in the square down by the wharves.

She looked a little undecided.

" What if I put on my shawl and went with you ! " she exclaimed. " Wait for me down below, Nikolai, so that we don't go together in the street up here ! "

It was a proposal that it was not easy to resist, she was so eager about it. And then he had been made foreman to-day !

She was not long in putting on her blue-striped dress and a shawl over her head and following him.

They hastened down together; she chattering gaily as in the old days when they had stolen out, he quite taken up with looking at and listening to her. They walked in the middle of the road, anything but carefully; clouds of dust arose at every step, but Nikolai only saw Silla, dark-eyed, warm and gay in the middle of it all.

Down in the town that warm summer evening,

the streets were unusually busy about the fish-place. There was evidently something that occasioned more life and movement than usual. The bridge was full of people hanging over the railings and looking down at all those who were pushing their way forwards amid noise, shouts and cries to get a mackerel for their supper.

This greenish-blue, shining fish, so round and strong and. quick, sea-built for lightning speed, its head formed for cleaving the water, and an elastic arrow-feather as the termination to an almost dangerously slender tail—it had already been glittering for two days on the stalls in the fish-market.

Even as late as yesterday morning it was a rarity, and only for the tables of the wealthier, but later in the afternoon another smack came in, —there had been a large haul out by the Hval Islands—and to-day two more loaded vessels, so that the market was over-stocked.

Yes, indeed, the mackerel had come—that is to say, the mackerel that the working-man can buy. It was to be had now for two-pence or two-pence halfpenny apiece, both on the fish-market and up the river here. The women, who speculated, carried them in baskets up to all the most out-of-the-way parts of the town.

It found its way now everywhere, where there was only a hole for it to slip into, a kettle or a pan for it to be boiled or fried in—into all the

galleys in the harbour, from the large, superior
steamship or full-rigged vessel, down to the cook-
ing-stoves on the timber sloops and the little
decked barges, where people were resting, and
broiling it in the summer evening, into all the
back blocks and small streets from the cellars to
the garrets. Workmen and small tradesmen, hus-
bands and wives were going that sultry evening
with one, two, or three in their hand, according
to the number of mouths there were at home.
There was a smell of fried and broiled mackerel
over whole quarters of the town.

It *must* be sold, it was so confoundedly hot!

"Yes, indeed, it is a blessed warmth," answered
deaf Mother Andersen, "that sends all this mackerel
over the town."

This fish has had a prejudice to overcome, although
in all modesty it has solicited nothing but the favour
of being allowed to escape being eaten. It has
the reputation of being the cannibal of the North
Sea—in plain words, a man-eater, and that the
dark part of its flesh comes from drowned sailors.

Nikolai and Silla were also down at the boats
to seize their share of the glory of the evening.
Silla had not lived near the wharves in her
childhood for nothing, and to pick out the best
fish from under the very nose of the old women,
was an easy matter for her. She stood eagerly
bargaining and stretching out over the boat.

"Thanks very much, mother, but you won't fool

me into taking that sunburnt mackerel skin ! Take
some of those that are lying behind there under
the thwart—those two—yes, just those."

She weighed them in her hand to see if they
were firm and stiff.

Nikolai's hand was already in his pocket; but
Silla threw the mackerel contemptuously into the
boat again.

" Why, they're as old as the hills ! Eyes as dead
as horn ! "

" Those beautiful——"

" Be quiet, Nikolai ! If we are to be satisfied
with these for supper, mother, you'll have to take off
a farthing or two."

In the end they went for two-pence a piece.

" What a fine trader you are, Nikolai ! " she said
to tease him, on the way home. " But do you see
how big and fresh they are ?"

Barbara was standing on the steps, shading her
eyes with her hand, and looking to see if Nikolai
were not soon coming with the fish.

The person she did see coming quietly and
sedately up the road was Silla, and she chatted with
her from the steps until Nikolai also at last appeared
with the two mackerel.

Of course Silla must come in and see how they
tasted; there was no question of Barbara's honour
and superabundant hospitality putting up with anything else.

In there on Barbara's cooking-stove the mackerel

hissed and broiled that light evening. The peculiar, rather pungent smell of frying grew stronger and more appetising as it went on.

Then the pieces had to be turned with fresh fat in the pan—fresh hissing!

The scent floated out through the open window, and far into the street.

Barbara was big and slow in turning, while Silla, quick and ready, put now one thing, now another into her hands, and hurried away, and was over the fish both with her face and her opinions, long before Barbara could collect herself.

Nikolai's broad, pleased face followed the whole of the frying process with deeply interested attention.

"That mackerel's the right sort of fellow for frying!"

And then at last to take the pieces straight from the pan on to the bread!

The evening breeze began to blow cool between the warm house walls. The three who sat there enjoying the mackerel, felt as if it were a festive night.

And foreman too!

CHAPTER XI

THE WEDDING POSTPONED AGAIN

CONFINED as she was, and made to work through the long evenings, while her mother watched her like an eagle, Silla's only chance of indemnifying herself was up at the factory.

She went about there with a suppressed longing and eager interest, her eyes sparkling, in the midst of all the chattering, whispering and gossiping among her different ideals—Kristofa and Gunda, active Swedish Lena, and pert Jakobina. If she could not be with them herself, she might at any rate hear what fun they had had, and all that had happened. In this way she could live their life at second hand.

It was of course Kristofa who knew how to put everything in a captivating, magic light. A little walk, a possible engagement, an evening at a dance, everything was moulded by her busy imaginative power into events that never wanted a hero, that interesting, mystic being, who was seen, now with a cigar, now without one, who sometimes pretended he did not know them, sometimes nodded, or only smiled. The person in question might be some town gentleman or other, or some one from one of the offices up there, who often had not the faintest suspicion that his coming and going was seen in Bengal illumination, or that it caused such a flutter in their hearts; though this did not preclude others from both suspecting and taking advantage of it.

These, through Kristofa's habit of spinning, grew into little romances, which Silla took in with wide-open eyes, and afterwards continued at home.

Silla herself had a little romance which she kept to herself: she would not dare to tell it to Nikolai.

She had to take care, when she went at dinner-time to buy anything for her mother at Barbara's, that Veyergang had not gone in there on his way down to light his cigar.

The last time she had met him there, he laughed and asked whether the black-eyed maid wanted to run away from him? He was not so very terrible! She had completely vanished lately. He had heard that her mother kept her in a cage for the sake of a dangerous smith—was that true? When a young girl had two such black eyes, she ought not to hide them away.

And yet it was not altogether a warlike condition; but he knew very well that she watched and waited, however long it might be, until he had left the shop.

All this was like a ray of sunlight through the high, barred paling.

In other respects, one day passed like another,

from the hum of the factory into the work at home, and Mrs. Holman was quite satisfied with the help she really must say she had of Silla this summer. That her daughter grew more large-eyed, pale and thin, it was not in her nature to attach much importance to ; it only showed that Silla was not accustomed to systematic work.

On the rare occasions when Nikolai had an opportunity of speaking to her, Silla complained sadly.

She talked herself into such exasperation that she cried over everything that the others—all the others —had leave to do, and only she had not. To begin with, in her childhood, and all the time she was growing up, she had been bottled up in that cellar in the square, and now, when she was grown up, she had got into a regular workhouse !

After having thought gloomily and sadly over this for a time, her reflections took another course, and she began to anticipate impetuously how they would amuse themselves, she and Nikolai, when once she got away from home. She would have fun like all other young people, even if they had to give a dance in their own room. And go out in a boat in the evening and row and fish, and on Sundays take their dinner out into the woods, and shout so loud that the hills would ring again.

She was almost wild, and her eyes burned with all the pressure and work that was put upon her.

When she did not get excited with talking, she looked depressed—more so every time, Nikolai

K

thought. Her face seemed to him to wear such a plaintive expression.

There was nothing to be done but to set his teeth and hammer away, and hope for release by the winter.

Georgina Korneliussen in the next house but one, who sewed uppers for the shoemaker—she was such a nice, quiet girl. Silla should make friends with her, Mrs. Holman thought ; it began to dawn upon her that there are limits to being trained in one's duty. On Sundays they might take it in turns to visit one another, for then they would be under surveillance in both places. And Mrs. Holman even allowed Silla one Sunday to go for a walk with Georgina down in the town. Young people must have a little pleasure now and then.

Silla had looked forward all the week to this Sunday with the passionate impatience of a bird that is to be let out of its cage, and the morning rose on great expectations of what the day would bring with it.

It seemed as if the soup with swedes in it would never be ready, so that they could have dinner. And afterwards there was endless waiting for Georgina, who could not finish adorning herself.

At last she came out, tightly laced, and with a strip of crochet in the neck of her dress. What sort of oil or fatty substance she had plastered down her hair with may be left unsaid ; but Silla in her brown straw hat and a plain white collar, felt for a moment insignificant beside her. But she quickly took her friend's arm; now they were off to amuse themselves!

Down to the town they went, Silla impatiently champing the bit in her desire to get there in time to take part in the day's pleasures.

In the streets and the park at this respectable time in the afternoon, crowds of people clad in their best were strolling up and down looking at one another, and for a long time Silla and Georgina had enough to do in directing one another's attention to the finest and most fashionable dresses, and especially the long white flowing scarfs wound under the chin and thrown over the shoulder. These, and white straw hats with light blue or pink ribbons and roses, were the objects of their vehement admiration.

They went up and down, lost sight of and met again the same dresses, and the same stiff quiet Sunday faces.

This was repeated until it became wearisome, and Silla proposed that they should go somewhere else, which, under Georgina's guidance, led to a walk round the fortress.

Nature was not their object; and they only met one or two tired, bored individuals who evidently did not know what to do with themselves on Sunday afternoon: now and then they stopped and looked up at the trees.

A sentry called his long-drawn "Relieve guard!"

It sounded like a mighty yawn in the afternoon. Out on the calm, shining fjord lay boats and vessels drifting in the breathless heat.

There was nothing here, so they made their way down to the harbour.

Here, too, was emptiness and Sunday desolation, the vessels seemed to have died out.

Another cruise up the street.

On the market-place stood some unemployed forces, who had found a Sunday amusement in exchanging watches,* while the bells of the church behind them were ringing in the congregation to evening service.

Tired, wearied, and thirsty, they continued their walk up the street until they came into the motley stream of people who were wending their way down to the piers, where the steamers were constantly coming in and going out with passengers from and to the islands.

Here a difference of opinion arose.

Georgina thought there were so many people, and perhaps it was not proper to go by the steamer, as it was beginning to grow late.

But Silla thought that they had swallowed dust in the streets long enough, and that they must make use of the little time they had. Was Georgina going home satisfied with the pleasure she had already had?

---

* In Norway this is a pastime often resorted to by men on holidays, when time hangs heavy on their hands. I have seen even old men deeply absorbed in the examination of each other's watches, with a view to their exchange.—*Trans.*

It was cool and airy sitting in the wind in the front of the boat and resting themselves after the fruitless roaming in the heat.

They went on shore from the crowded steamboat to the island, where the people gradually dispersed along the various shady walks.

Close to the way up from the pier, and commanding a view of the bay, stood the great place of amusement, with all its gates invitingly open, and the sound of dance-music floating out. Within was life and merriment.

Silla stopped to look in and listen to the music, but Georgina, highly scandalised, pulled her on.

Was that the place for a respectable girl to stop?

Silla followed slowly; there was inspiriting dance-music brightening all the path within the wooden paling, and she drank it in with both ears, while the rhythm rocked in her veins.

A little higher up, where the path turned off, she stopped again; she could not leave the music, and scandalised Georgina by going right up to the paling and trying to see in.

Georgina would leave her that very minute! She ought to have so much respect for herself as not to stand there! *She* had, at any rate, and cared too much for her good name even to want to listen to such a noise, and would go a long way round to avoid it.

She was extremely indignant.

Silla could really not comprehend how it could take the gloss off either of them if they stood there a little and listened; nor yet what they had come out for. Just where there was a little life and gaiety they were to shut their eyes and put their fingers in their ears. But where it was so "nice and proper" it had not been particularly amusing; and she would give her a new sixpence if Georgina could tell her of a "proper" amusement when they had a holiday: they had been searching for one now both long and carefully.

She sauntered on.

According to Georgina, there was still nice time before the evening traffic to the place of amusement began, and they spent it in diverse walks in the roads, though never so far that they could not keep an eye on the steamers and be standing in good time among the crowd that was thronging the pier.

Tired, cross and footsore, they at last reached home late in the evening, where Silla, in the middle of the account she was giving her mother of all the places they had been to, fell asleep in her chair.

The music was running in her head, and she dreamt she was at a ball.

* * * *

There was a pleasant crackling in the stove at Barbara's in the chilly autumn days, when people who could not afford it so well were loth to begin fires.

It was, therefore, very comfortable to stand about at her counter talking, and still more so for the chosen few who were fortunate enough to be invited to partake of a cup of coffee.

But of late Barbara had not been nearly so even-tempered as formerly. She suffered from change-ableness of spirits, was sometimes unnaturally stingy, so that it looked as if she wanted to count the groats or the coffee-beans, at other times in a different mood, open-handed and liberal to both guests and customers.

Whatever the reason might be, it was certain that now and then in quiet moments she would fall into a brown study. The bill for sugar, meal, flour and coffee had come in again.

The till was anything but prepared for such an achievement; it groaned and rattled whatever time in the day she pulled it out or pushed it in.

Time, however, went on inexorably, notwithstanding that the stove roared so cheerfully as if nothing were the matter.

And it had now gone so far that the day after to-morrow was the day for payment.

Barbara was in a—for her—most unnatural state of excitement. In the hope of obtaining a very last, further postponement, she had this afternoon carried out her long contemplated attack on the salesman down in his office, but had met with a decided refusal. If she did not pay now, after all she had promised, then—well, then, after the answer she received, it looked as if the wheel would suddenly come to a standstill.

It was this that Barbara, going feverishly in and out, with her best bonnet still loosely tied upon her

head, was explaining to Nikolai, who was sitting
in the kitchen.

Nikolai's face did not look as if he saw any help
for it. On the contrary, he sat bending forward
with compressed lips, looking down at the floor and
twirling his thumbs. His hair as well as the
position of his shoulders and his whole expression
looked combative.

Barbara sat down by the cooking-stove ; she drew a
heavy breath, and sighed out of an oppressed breast.

It would come to an execution as sure as she
lived—and it was for thirty-eight dollars !

Nikolai knew well what she was coming to, and
that she was only waiting for him to give her a
word that she could hang on to ; but this money
that he had scraped together was held much faster.
He knew what he wanted, and this trade was only
going farther and farther backwards, in any case.

Barbara groaned. She might as well go into the
black ground at once.

Nikolai only snapped his fingers and looked down,
doubly decided, at the crack in the floor.

When the pause had become unbearable any
longer, and she saw clearly that no answer was
coming, she began to cry softly.

She *had* thought, she sobbed, that when she had
a son who was a smith's foreman, she would not
stand quite helpless in the world.

"You know, mother, how badly I am in want of
money myself."

Again an obstinate silence, with continued sobbing and drying of eyes on Barbara's side.

"It might be as well to consider whether the shop really paid?" suggested Nikolai at last cautiously.

"Would he like her to give up like a cow to be slaughtered before Christmas," she exclaimed angrily —"and no more money than that was!"

"I only meant it would be better to stop in time."

But these words had the effect of fire on gunpowder. She got up, as red as a tile. Just so! Now *he* wanted her to close!

She rushed—in a manner somewhat recalling the useful animal just mentioned by herself, when it is trying to get loose—into the shop and back again.

If Nikolai thought that she would give up and go bankrupt to be jeered at by everybody, when she only needed to go down and borrow that little of Ludvig, he was very much mistaken.

Barbara was quite flushed.

She would not let herself be ruined a second time for Nikolai's sake. It was quite enough that he had injured her welfare once before in this world. Yes, he need not sit and look at her with open mouth. What else was she turned out of the Veyergangs' house for, where she had been so important, if it was not because Nikolai had lifted his hand against the Consul-General's Ludvig. Oh yes, he might wonder as much as he liked, but that was why she had been driven out helpless into the world, from comfortable circumstances. And then when an opportunity came for Nikolai to support her a little, he had some one else to spend his money upon.

But the most vexatious part of it was that Nikolai also wanted to forbid her to apply to one who was as good as her own child, when there was the necessity for it.

She would pay no attention to that however. If *he* would not help her, he must put up with her going to one who could, now that it was a question of closing the shop and the whole business.

No, she swore she would not go bankrupt. And she struck the table so that the coppers danced in the drawer.

It was a good thing that it was this week, for next week he was going abroad for two or three months; he had said so himself yesterday, so that both she and Silla heard it.

Nikolai sat quite pale. His mouth moved as if it were trembling, and he wiped his forehead once or twice with his sleeve.

He looked slowly up at his mother; it was as if he were afraid of getting to hate her.

"You shall have the money."

He felt he was on the point of bursting into tears, and must get away to have his rage out.

It was another postponement for him and Silla until the spring. And where was the end of it to be?

His hand shook and fumbled with the door-handle.

This fresh piece of information, which his mother had so unexpectedly given Nikolai, that it was he who had destroyed her well-being, was like yet another stone weighing him down.

It crushed him like a moral defeat. He could not rid himself of the thought that there was something in it. He felt his courage was weakened, and he went about disheartened.

He had lost another quarter as to his prospects of getting married, and if his mother required or rather claimed money from him again for her down-hill trade, what could he do?

It was like work without hope, and despondency began to take hold of him.

When he put his shillings away in the tin box on Saturday, it was with bitter thoughts. At any moment his mother might come and swallow the whole of it—as she, of course, had a right to do, since he in his time had wasted all hers.

He had always thought that when it came to the point, it was he who had a reckoning to demand of his mother, because she had brought him into the world without being able to give him a father, and then let him go.

But now it seemed to be just the other way. His mother, with her all-consuming business, was the great, lawful gulf for all his happiness.

He began to be weary of it all.

Amid all this there sometimes dawned and smouldered a faint glow of rebellion within him, although, in his honest endeavour to come to the bottom of the truth, it was some time before it blazed up.

Should he let Silla go, too, into this same gulf?

The answer blazed up clearly, so that the flames shone and flickered:

"Not while there was a rag left of what was called Nikolai!"

And with reference to his mother, and his having perhaps brought misfortune upon her, should he not have hit out, but just let himself be insulted and trampled upon, as he was going to be again now? His mother, tall and big, would just squeeze them to death with that shop, both he and Silla. They were not even to have leave or the right to sigh.

But he would not have that.

He had thrashed Veyergang, and only repented that he had not hit harder. As he had come into the world, he would be a human being, even if he were to have his head cut off for it afterwards.

The shop up there should not be fattened with another penny out of the tin box. If his mother ever came to want for food, she would always find a place in his room; but that she should put a stop to his ever getting a room of his own—no, thank you!

He was like another man when he had at last made this clear to himself. Yes, his name was Nikolai, and he was foreman at Mrs. Ellingsen's.

CHAPTER XII

THE FAIR AND THE CONVICT

THE winter was passing.

It was at the time of the fair in the beginning of February. The streets swarmed with people and the snow in the thaw had turned to powdered sugar with the traffic.

A motley row of stalls stretched from market-place to market-place. Trumpets brayed, buffoons shouted, the lottery-wheel went round, the cryers howled. Music filled the air in volleys of blustering flourishes, and amidst it all, over the whole town, pleasure-seeking, dancing and merriment, until far on into the night.

Dull noise and the sound of music penetrated up to the manufacturing part of the town. In the evenings the town lay beneath it in increased illumination.

There was a kind of intoxication in the air, and there was many an impatient, longing soul up there of such as look severely upon themselves, while plenty of the looser sort streamed down.

From year to year the accounts grew of the large

fair-balls, of the trumpets, the coloured lamps in the
garden, and the matadores who stood treat.   It was
tempting and attractive.

As early as the second day Kristofa came, excited
and eager, with a solution of the question as far as
she and Gunda and Silla were concerned—money for
tickets and cakes too, for all three !

She behaved most mysteriously, talked all the
time of a certain person, whom she dared not, for all
the world, mention.

Silla had never before been to anything of the
kind, the most she had ever done was to stand outside among the longing crowd, who had to content
themselves with looking at the coloured lamps and
listening to the music.   Now at last there was a
chance for her too.

Oh, if she dared !

She was restless the whole morning, and had two
round red spots of colour on her cheeks.

At dinner-time her mother came up tired and out
of breath from the town.

She had had to promise the Antonisens to stand
at their cake-stall on the market-place through the
fair-week and help sell.   It was hardly-earned money
in the cold there and in the middle of all that shouting and bawling; but she would do her duty, and
not swerve from it when there was a penny to earn.
It would not be closed and packed up before mid-
night, so she must stay down there these few nights.

There was a buzzing and singing in Silla's ears;

it was as if the door were opening to her of itself. She could go now if she liked.

She was almost frightened.

As she was taking some washing home in the afternoon, down the street, young Veyergang suddenly brushed close by her.

She almost screamed ; then he had come back !

She dared not look up, and felt herself turn red, but had a momentary impression that he smiled and looked steadily at her and then nodded.

She knew the delicate scent of his cigar, and had a feeling that his clothes creaked, as it were, when he moved—a peculiarity which was connected with the romantic ideas of distinguished gentlemen that Kristofa had awakened in her.

It was he, she was quite sure now, who had given them the tickets.

Her heart beat and fluttered within her like a disturbed and frightened bird.

She went home in a reverie, so that at last Mrs. Holman had to ask if she were out of her mind.

She stole a glance into the looking-glass over the drawers.

Her eyes, were they so very black ? The freckles were still there. There was a cure for freckles—but there were *not* so many as there looked to be ; the old glass was so full of spots and holes in the quicksilver.

Mrs. Holman, to her surprise, saw Silla standing and rubbing, breathing on and polishing the mirror. Her daughter must have been seized with a new zeal.

On the evening of the third day of the fair, Nikolai strolled up to the factory district by lamplight.

He had been fairing on his own account, and had bought a workbox as a surprise for Silla—one with looking-glass inside the lid—and this afternoon he had put some mounting and a nice lock upon it.

He could surely in some way succeed in meeting her and showing it to her—so easily and with such a spring the lock went! And scissors and needle case he had put inside. She should have the key in her own keeping, and he would keep the box.

He had tied it in a handkerchief and put two cakes on the top, so that the person who could guess that it was anything but a workman's bundle that he was carrying would be more than clever.

He passed close beneath his mother's windows where there was a light, and peeped in to see if Silla might happen to be standing at the counter, and then strolled about indifferently up and down the streets.

It was so strangely deserted and empty here this evening.

And, look as he would through the gate and the paling, it was not possible for him to discover a light in Mrs. Holman's window.

After having exhausted every artifice, he stationed himself on the watch for a long time where the roads crossed and one went up to the Valsets' cottage.

But fortune did not favour him this evening; he remained standing there with his work-box.

It was dark all down the street except near the lamp-post.

There was somebody! There she was!

He hurried up.

No, it was that Jakobina Silla had been so much with in the summer.

There would at any rate be no harm in asking her.

"Isn't Mrs. Holman at home this evening?" he asked, taking off his cap.

"No; she's down at the fair, helping sell."

The inference flashed with a passionate joy upon Nikolai; then he would be able to go in and see Silla.

"And so, when the cat's away the mice will play," continued Jakobina. It was pretty well known that the smith came there for Silla's sake, and her vexation at her three friends having got tickets, and not her, filled her with spiteful gaiety. "Silla has taken a little trip into the town, too!" she added, laughing.

"Silla!"

"Yes, why shouldn't she? Mrs. Holman is sitting in the cold down there at a stall, kicking and stamping her feet; why shouldn't her daughter do the same at the fair ball?"—Jakobina was great at saying witty things—"especially when she perhaps has some one who will both dance with her and treat her," she said, letting off another shot, as Nikolai seemed to be struck dumb.

"Who's put that lie into your head, girl?"

L

"If I'm lying, so's Kristofa; and that Silla went down with her and Gunda a couple of hours ago I saw with my own eyes. The one I mean can afford to give fair-tickets to either three or six. But perhaps they were going to a prayer-meeting," she added, winking with one eye.

"What nonsense are you talking! You'd better take care what you say!" he exclaimed angrily.

"Ha, ha!" she laughed; "you're not such a stranger to him—he's almost related. We're so grand, we are! We heard enough of that from your mother last summer, when she got him to pay for that fine black dress, and they wouldn't let her have credit for any more sewing materials for her shop."

Nikolai had heard enough.

His mother had wrung his very blood from him, and then—deceived him in spite of it.

He suddenly saw her before him in the cold light of indifference.

She had never been a mother to him, had never cared a pin's head about him! All this about a mother had only been something he had imagined.

He made a movement with his hands as if he were done with her. The one she cared about, and had a mother's feeling for, was this—

He did not know whether he had thought the name himself, or whether Jakobina had said it; but it rang in his ears like the stroke of a hammer on a shining anvil, as he rushed down:

"Ludvig Veyergang!"

He had robbed him of his mother from his earliest childhood. Was he going to drag Silla away from him too?

The thought at last became too impossible, and he slackened his pace.

That Jakobina was always so full of gossip and lies! This about Silla was all nonsense! There was nothing so dreadful in the three girls having taken a trip down to see a little of the fair; and they made that sharp-tongued Jakobina, whom they did not want to have with them, think they were all three going to the ball.

He, he, he! it was Silla who had thought of that! He would tell her he had seen that at once as soon as she told him.

He shook his head; for a moment he felt immensely re-assured, and relapsed into the bitter thoughts about his mother.

But—it would not be so out of the way if he went and looked for them; they might have taken it into their heads to stand outside and listen to the music.

The kettle-drums at the place of amusement were rattling out delight far into the air. From the menagerie close by brayed a shrieking trumpet, and the street outside was black with people.

It is not easy to say why it should have been so, but uneasiness again took possession of him.

In the illuminated entrance the strings and lines of lamps shone with an uncertain light in the raw gusty evening air; whole and half lines grew dim and almost went out, and then flared up again with a glare over the snow and the inpouring streams of people.

He could only advance at a foot's pace here; but while he slowly worked his way in, he looked all round. He only needed to see the outline of the figure he was looking for.

She was not among the people standing outside.

It was almost tiresome, now he had made up his mind he should see her.

He began to think of going to the booths to look for her there, and his glance wandered indifferently over the people.

She?—that rosy, laughing girl in there in the garden, with the round hat and the bit of boa round her neck over her jacket, was no other than Gunda!

He held his breath, as if he expected the next moment to see others in the crowd there among the lamps.

"Have you a ticket? Garden or ball?" he was asked at the entrance.

Nikolai would like to have taken tickets for the whole thing; but the pence he had about him were only enough for the garden.

The row of lamps lighted up the snowy road to a crowded restaurant, from the first floor windows of which came the shrieks of a woman's soprano, followed every now and then by a storm of applause. Farther on, a roundabout, crammed with people, was going round under an illuminated roof to the accompaniment of shrill music.

On both sides was a moving and, as regards the male portion, very miscellaneous and mixed crowd of fair-frequenters.

He searched the garden through, but in the darker paths outside the principal one, only a few loitering, shivering figures were to be seen, who seemed hovering like longing moths about the light.

It was down in that building, from which came sounds of music, the one to which all the people streamed and stood in a dense crowd outside, that the ball was going on.

All the blood in him seemed suddenly to stand still, and he approached slowly and hesitatingly, his face grey with apprehension.

He stood outside for a long time, gazing in at the large, lighted windows. Dark shadows passed behind the blinds, an unceasing variety of heads and shoulders.

There where the blind was pulled a little to one side he saw the round-headed Gunda again; the back of her head was so near him that he would have liked to push the pane in and ask her where Silla was?

He felt the shaking of the floor and the music twice as much where he was standing; it was as if the whole ball had got into his head.

Now he caught a glimpse of a sloping shoulder and half a back in an overcoat, with a cane sticking out of the owner's pocket—and part of a fashionable hat-brim.

The figure was smoking a cigar and bending down as if to talk.

To whom ?—To whom ?

For it was Ludvig Veyergang's, that narrow, straight back, that seemed in its pride as if it could not bend above the hips.

And then that way with his arm and his eyeglass.

Now he was gone ; he must be dancing.

The clear glimpse he could get through the little opening in the blind was dimmed by moisture. Only when a heavy drop ran down the pane in the heat inside, could he catch a fraction of a glimpse through the streak.

There came Veyergang's shadow, with stick and hat again, and lower down the crooked outline of a woman's head in lively gesticulation.

Again the figure with the stick disappeared, and Nikolai prepared to watch for it.

A drop just wept a smooth streak down the pane, and the next moment he caught a glimpse of a dancing figure—only a bent head and a half-hidden face.

He had seen enough—more than if he had had a hundred chandeliers to see by.

Immediately after, Nikolai was in the stream in front of the door.

It opened and closed incessantly to admit those who gave up tickets, and disclosed, in misty perspective, a miscellaneous confusion of hot, flushed faces.

Now and then a pair came out and hastened up to the large restaurant.

He heard both exclamations and taunts.

"Now then! now then!" came from the crowd.

Nikolai only worked his way towards the door. If once he stood there——!

"Ticket?"

Nikolai did not answer.

"Ticket, man? Ticket?"

Nikolai only pressed boldly a step nearer.

The police-constable made a movement, but met a look in Nikolai's face which made him feel justified in restraining himself. This pertinacious, silent working man looked as though he could strike.

The door continued to open and shut as incessantly as before, and both the constable and the ticket collector had become in a measure reconciled to the man who stood there so persistently—it almost looked as if he had a lawful business there, with that bundle in his hand—when Nikolai suddenly put his smith's shoulder to the door and pressed violently against it.

The ticket collector resisted in vain with his body; his hands were occupied.

Through the opening Nikolai had seen Silla, red, laughing, and out of breath with dancing, coming down the room with Ludvig Veyergang; he was looking about short-sightedly, with his hat pressed down sideways over his forehead and his eye-glass in one eye, with light arrogance, as if he were only going about his lawful business, when he was ruining a young girl.

There was a noise and disturbance down at the door.

"Turn him out! Turn him out!"

At last the cry sounded over the whole room. It was an interlude, during which the audience climbed up on to tables and benches to try to see.

Nikolai would blindly and roughly have forced his way in, had not the police officer met him at the door, and with his own and the constable's united efforts managed to drag the strong, unruly smith out.

His one thought, while with a certain cool, temperate leniency they dragged him out into the half-darkness, was to keep so near that he could have an eye on the door. He felt with suppressed rage that if they drove him to it, he would sooner die than leave the garden now.

The music ceased. A number of people, hot and breathless, streamed out during a pause in the dancing.

There came Veyergang—and Silla, bashful and half-resisting, with him. They took the way up to the restaurant.

Nikolai suddenly disengaged himself with a jerk, and the next moment, emerging from the darkness, thrust himself between them.

Silla uttered a cry of terror, but Nikolai only gave her a half-glance, and flung her behind him—and thus stood face to face with Veyergang.

The young lion changed colour and retreated a step before the expression of violent hatred confronting him ; but, recognising the old enemy of his school days, he curled his lip scornfully.

That look made Nikolai rush upon him, and Veyergang, with a cry of " You cowardly ruffian ! " returned the blow with his walking-stick right across Nikolai's face, so that the stick snapped.

" Help ! help ! Police ! "

Nikolai had struck his fist into Veyergang's chest so that the buttons of his coat were torn open, when he was surrounded by three policemen.

A young girl suddenly rushed wildly in among them.

Spectators collected in greater numbers around.

This was a fair-fight of the first sort ; and that tall, dark girl too !

" A mad bull-dog of a smith ! Put him under arrest ! " exclaimed Veyergang furiously, when he felt himself in safety. " You may meditate there in the meantime. You are not at all indispensable, my friend ! " he went on in a coolly teasing tone. " The black-eyed lassie shall enjoy herself at the fair all the same."

The words were hardly spoken before Nikolai had wrenched himself free. He swung the bundle, with the box in it, about him so that nobody could come near him, and darted like a flash of lightning upon Veyergang, exclaiming between his teeth :

"It's the last time in your life that you'll say that!"

One hand fumbled with Veyergang's coat, and the other dealt him a blow with the full weight of the box, so that he fell backwards on to the snow.

He did not get up again—did not stir.

There were cries and a tumult among the spectators. Some cried "Murder," others for a doctor. And all the while the music clashed and jingled in three directions.

A high police functionary attempted to quiet the excitement, and discreet hands bore the unconscious man out to a sledge, and drove him to the hospital. All the excited wrath of the crowd was turned against the perpretrator of the deed, who was led out strongly guarded.

For safety's sake, out in the gate, irons were put on both his hands and his feet, and this was done in the midst of an ever-increasing crowd from the street.

But when there was a mention of taking him into the sledge, the girl threw herself upon him, and clung so tightly that it was impossible to tear her away. She still cried and clung to him, much to the delight and amusement of the assembled crowd of boys, after they had got him into the sledge.

It was impossible for them to start, although they dragged and pulled at her till the gathers of her dress gave way.

The boys shouted.

" Pull—tear—drag the clothes off my back ! "

" There, have a little common-sense, lass ! " said one of the constables."

" You mustn't take him ! You sha'n't take him ! "

She wrenched and pulled at his hand-cuffs.

" It's my fault ! Can't you tell them so, Nikolai ? " she cried piercingly, and the policemen took the opportunity to detach her hands.

The sledge dashed off, and Silla, without a shawl, after it, followed by a swarm of boys.

She saw the door of the police-station open for Nikolai without being able to reach him or hinder it ; hour after hour she passed outside, listening and waiting, while the constables again and again intimated to her that she must go home.

When at length she wandered away in despair, she kept stopping ; but up on the bridge over the waterfall she stood still a long while.

It roared so strangely down there in the dark. It seemed as if in some way or other she belonged to it.

All night she lay with a dull feeling of what had happened, and writhed under an unspeakable terror for the result of Nikolai's act.

Now and then she groaned out a suffering sigh.

She could not get rid of the sight of the hand-cuffs, and in her delirium felt the cold iron still in her hands, until at last the bitter feeling came over her of how miserably she had behaved to him. She felt as though the thought of her must make Nikolai sick.

She lay staring at herself as in a vision—how she had gone about and never thought or cared about anything but her own pleasure, while Nikolai, her smith boy, with the strong arms and the true eyes, who now sat behind the prison bolts, had striven and toiled, and saved, and worked for both of them, so that they might be together.

And she could see too, now, all at once, as if scales had fallen from her eyes, that he had been terribly afraid for her.

If only he still cared for her! He had said: " Go home, Silla "—twice—so kindly and gently, that she began to cry when she thought of it.

Had she known or understood what it was to love anybody before just now? And perhaps it was too late!

The thought filled her with despair again, and wild pictures arose in her mind—Veyergang falling and lying stretched upon the snow, and then Nikolai's arms with the handcuffs on them stretching up out of the factory waterfall.

She lay awake until the morning and saw the same things—the handcuffs in the waterfall, and Veyergang turning away from the blow and falling; and then the whole thing over again—and again.

She sat there the whole day until dusk. Then her restlessness drove her down to the police-station.

There the gas was already lighted in the passages, and there were so many doors through which busy men in uniform were going in and out. At the entrances several people were standing waiting.

She had not the courage to ask.

For a long time she walked restlessly in the thickly-falling snow round the building.

At last she felt that she must go in; and in a condition which made her blind to her surroundings, she at length stood patiently, white and covered with snow, at the gate of the prison.

When at length it opened, she wanted to go in.

"What do you want?"

"To hear about Nikolai."

"Nikolai? What Nikolai?"

"He who came in here last night."

"You don't mean him, the murderer? Are you his sister?"

"No."

"*That's* a good thing, for the bad fellow hasn't got long to live." He made an expressive movement with his hand across his throat. "The man he attacked is dead—died at midday, and the murderer is now sitting in chains."

Silla did not know how it was that the door was shut behind her again, and did not feel that it was snowing thickly and silently, while the light from the lamps shone through a veil of snow—did not know how she had reached the bridge again.

That was where she ought to be.

Nikolai was sitting down there with handcuffs on, and stretching up his hands, and crying—crying to her!

The next morning a bit of a dress was seen sticking

up out of the loose snow in the dam. Her skull had
been broken in the high fall from the bridge against
the edge of the ice.

*   *   *   *

It was proved that young Veyergang's death had
been caused directly by the blow that had been dealt
him which had penetrated to the brain.

And the impression was not to be softened by
Nikolai's behaviour before the court. He stood there
with wild sorrow in his heart over Silla's death, and
answered that if Veyergang had had seven lives, he
would have taken them all.

When questioned as to his parents, he at first
declared that he had never known any; but when
pressed further, he exclaimed, pointing at a large-
boned woman who was sitting, crying on a bench :

" Her name is Barbara. They say she is my
mother ; but he who took away my happiness in this
world got both her affection and her mother's milk."

Barbara wailed.

His father ? It might be the whole town !—he
looked round on the officials of the court.

This was an answer which fully confirmed the
opinion which had been general from the first in this
horrible, sensational murder case—that the court
had here before it a bold criminal nature, early
hardened in the dregs of town life.

The police still had a pretty clear remembrance
of this individual from his violent conduct and other
doubtful circumstances under a charge of theft.
And it appeared from his past life, which was

thoroughly sifted, that from his earliest childhood he had evinced dangerous tendencies, so that there had even been talk of placing him in an asylum for depraved children.

There were repeated facts brought forward from the time of his apprenticeship in Hægberg's smithy, which proved that he was an individual given to fighting and violence.

Not longer ago than last year he had threatened Olaves' life, or so the witnesses interpreted it ; and it appeared in the examination in court, that on the evening in question he had persistently plotted against the deceased, and had, just before the perpetration of the deed, declared his murderous intention in the threat : " It's the last time in your life that you'll say that ! "

There was undeniably an extenuating circumstance in the fact that there was a love-story connected with the affair, and that the act seemed to be prompted by jealousy. On the other hand, it was clearly shown that it might also be considered as the outcome of an old hatred existing even in the years of their childhood.

The sentence of imprisonment with hard labour for life was passed.

*　　　*　　　*　　　*

There was rifle-practice going on, puff after puff, down in the moat. Further along, on the green, some soldiers were being drilled, and now and again a trumpet signal sounded out on the still morning air.

Under a guard of overseers a little band of

fettered prisoners was being conducted, with a clanking echo at every step, along the ramparts from their work towards the inner building of the convict prison.

At a hole in the wall the last of the prisoners slackened his pace a little. He cast a lingering glance through the opening.

The fjord lay shining blue beneath, with its many white sails and a steamer leaving a thick trail of smoke behind it on the water.

He drew a deep breath, his nostrils expanded, and there were signs of great agitation in his broad face.

The others were already five or six steps in advance, and the overseer began to roar at Number 66, exclaiming morosely:

" You'd give something to be able to fly out now, Nikolai! "

" I think that's the way we're all made! " he answered quickly.

" Then you should try and behave so as to get a remission."

Nikolai shook his head bitterly; a gleam shot from his grey eyes.

" If I got out, it would only be to come in again. For either the world ought to go to prison or I ought, and I suppose it may as well be the last! "

The clanking went on again.

Printed by BALLANTYNE, HANSON & Co
London & Edinburgh

www.ingramcontent.com/pod-product-compliance
Lightning Source LLC
Chambersburg PA
CBHW022356020726
47500CB00002B/307